Victorian Fashion
coloring book
by Anna Nadler

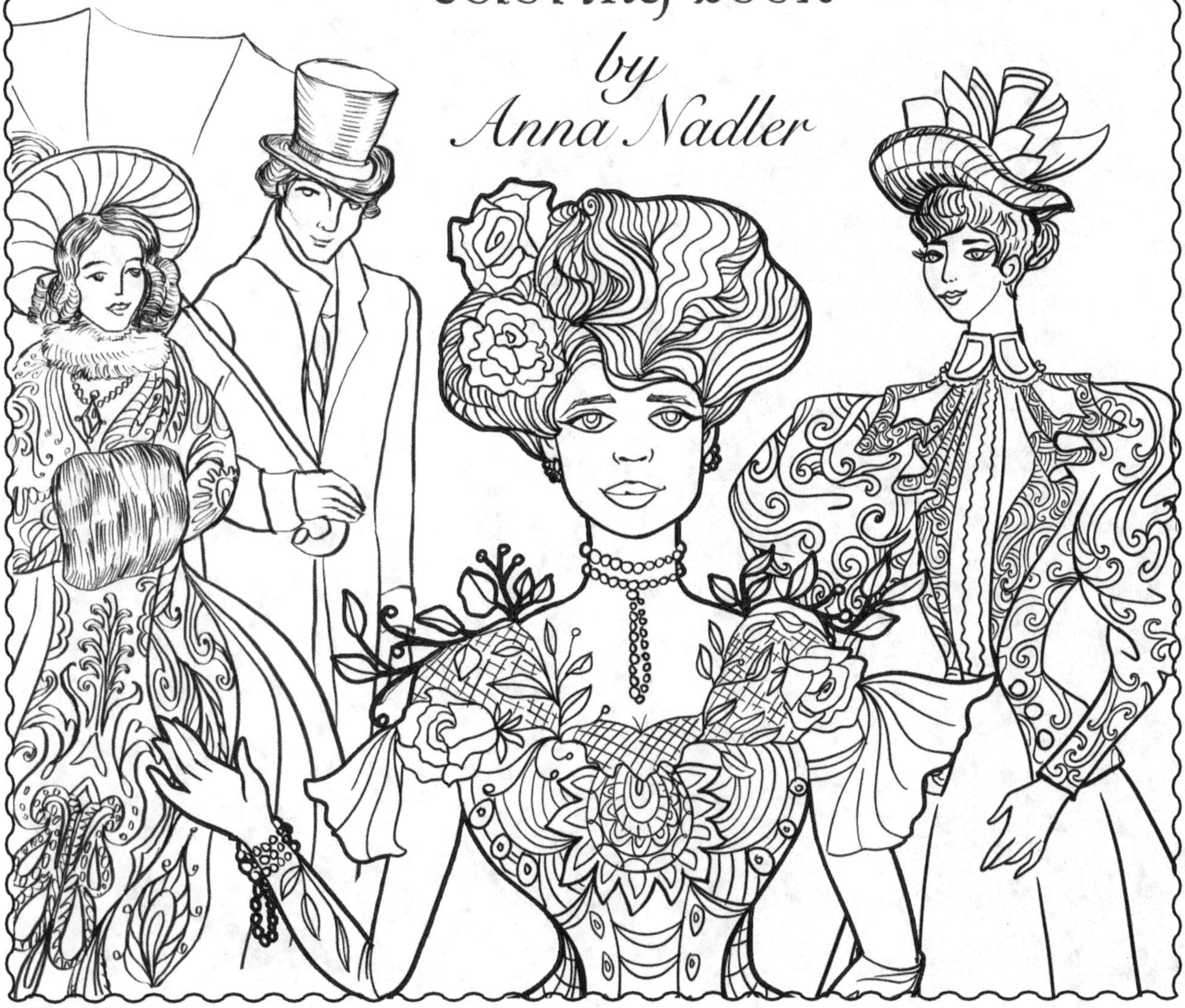

Copyright © 2021 Anna Nadler
All rights reserved
Published by Little Birdie Press™
No part of this publication may be
reproduced, stored in a retrieval system or
transmitted in any form or by any means,
electronic, mechanical, photocopying, recording
or otherwise, without prior written permission
from the author/publisher.
www.annanadler.com

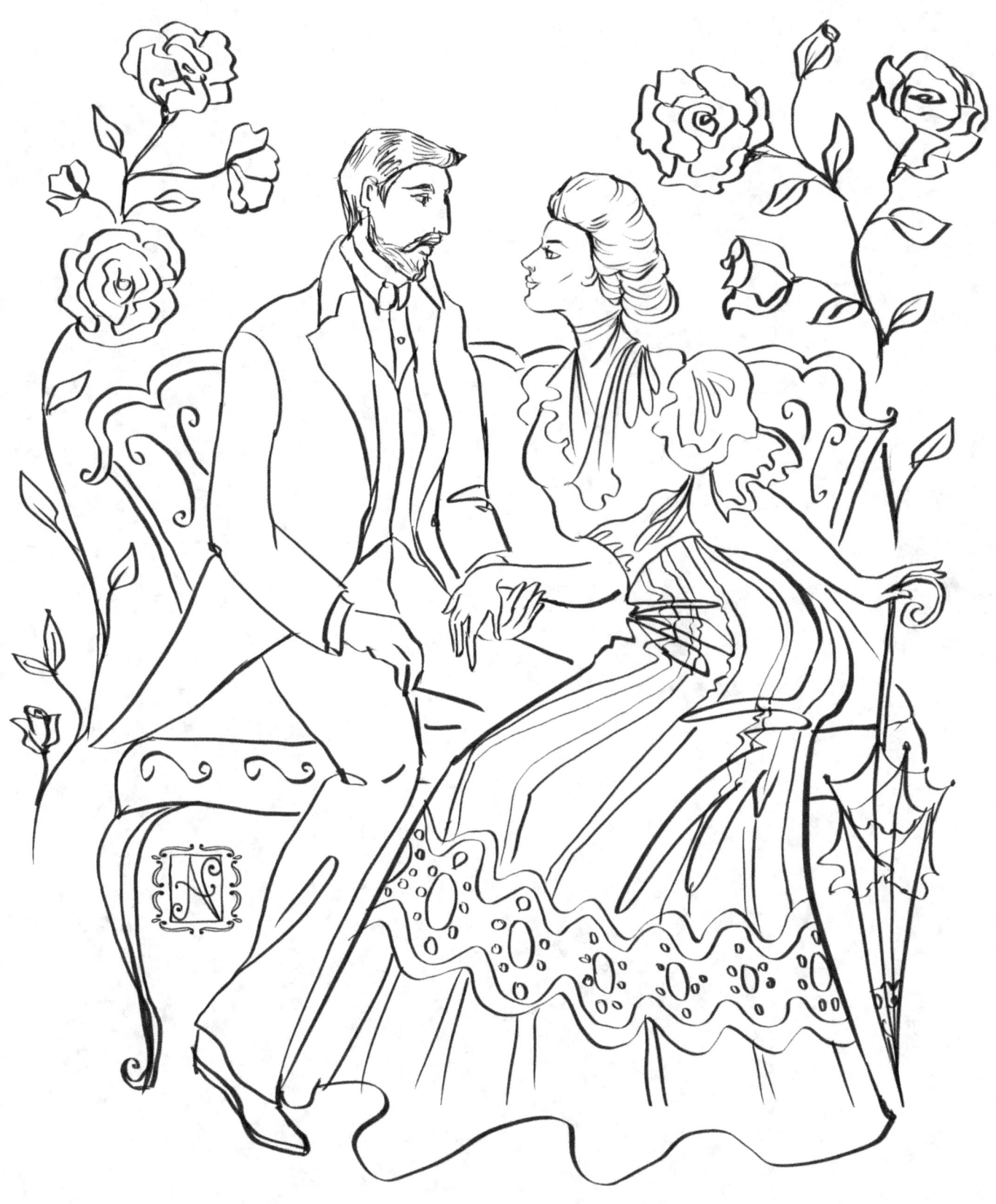

"It is happy for you that you possess the talent of flattering with delicacy."

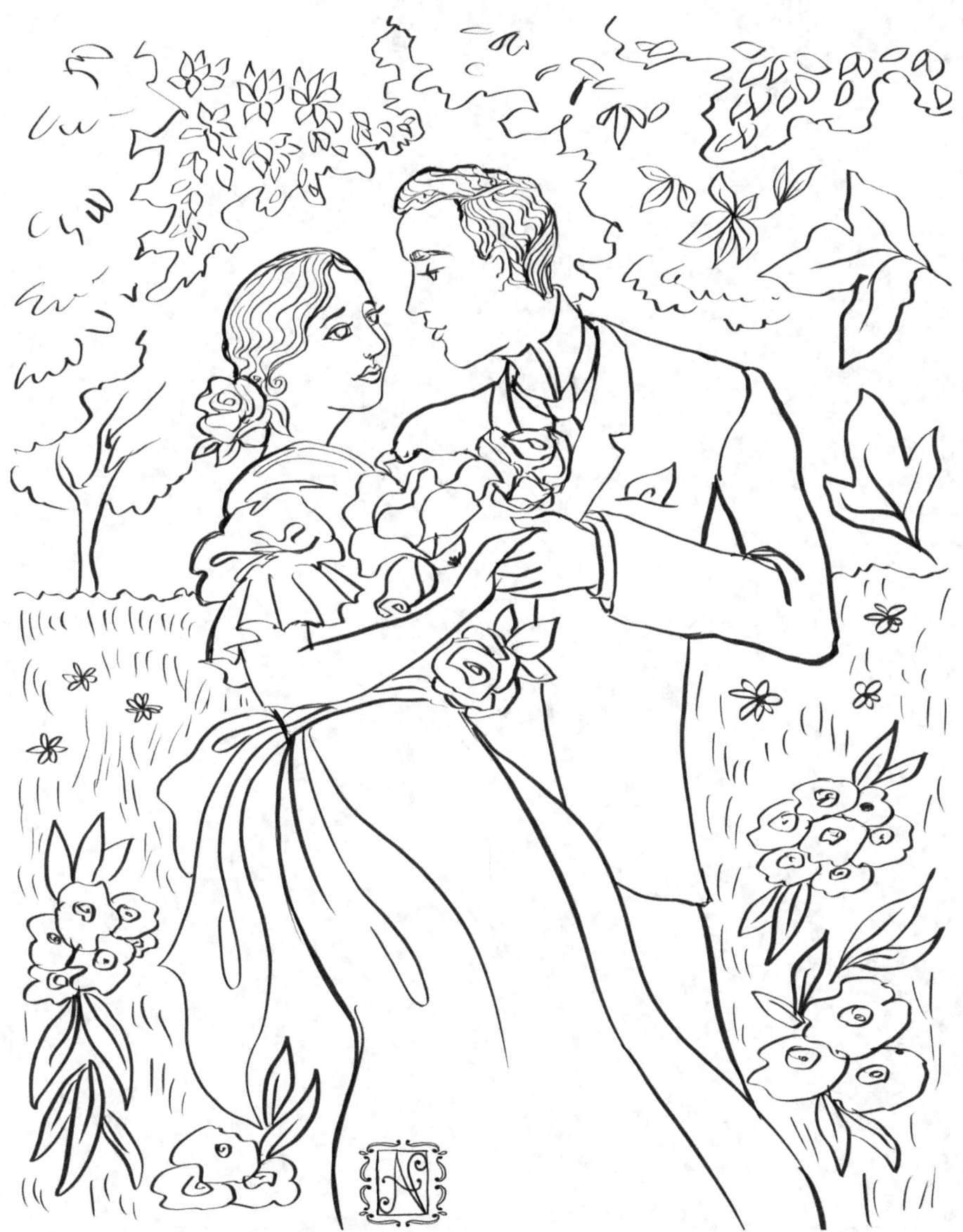

"Is not general incivility the very essence of love?"

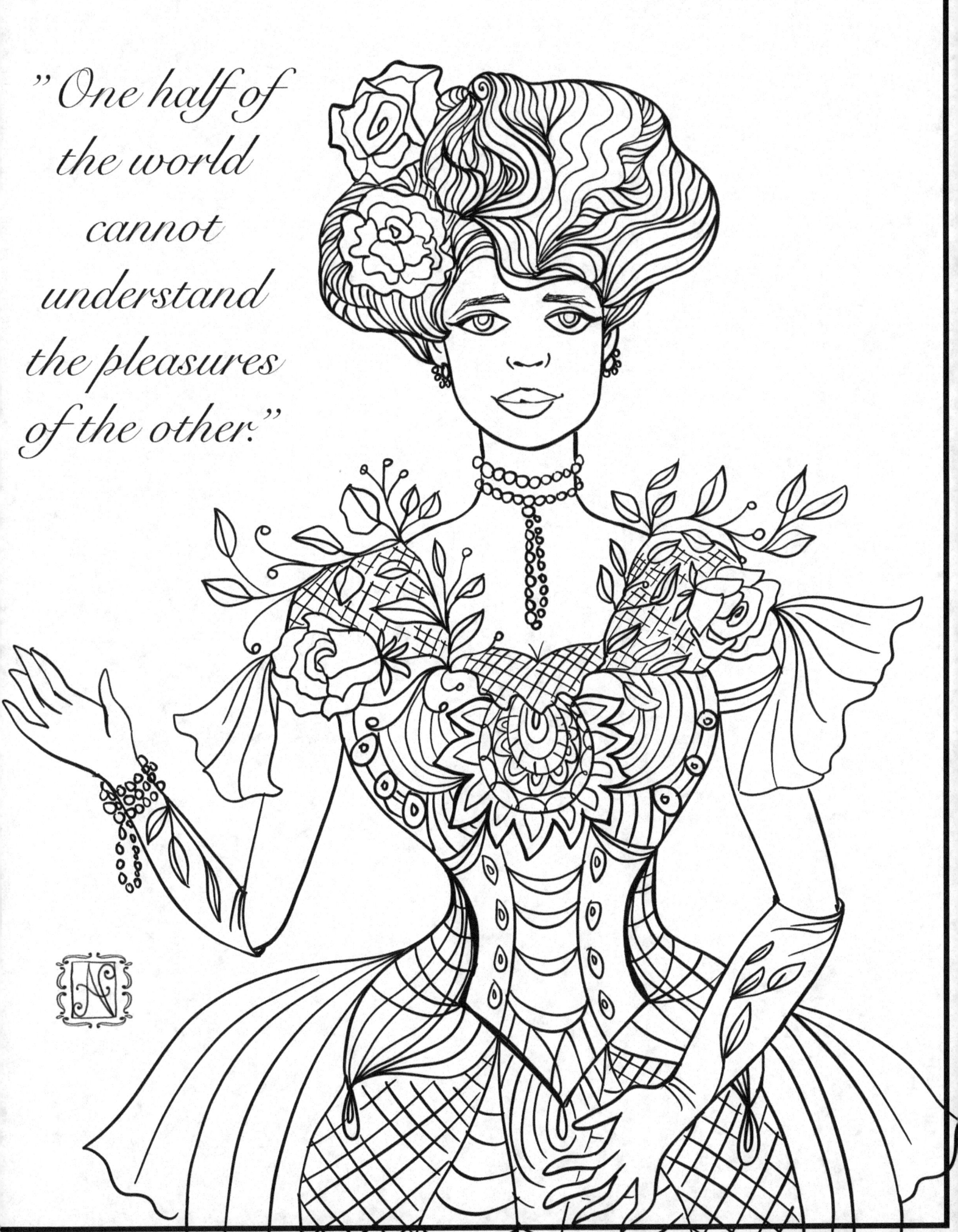

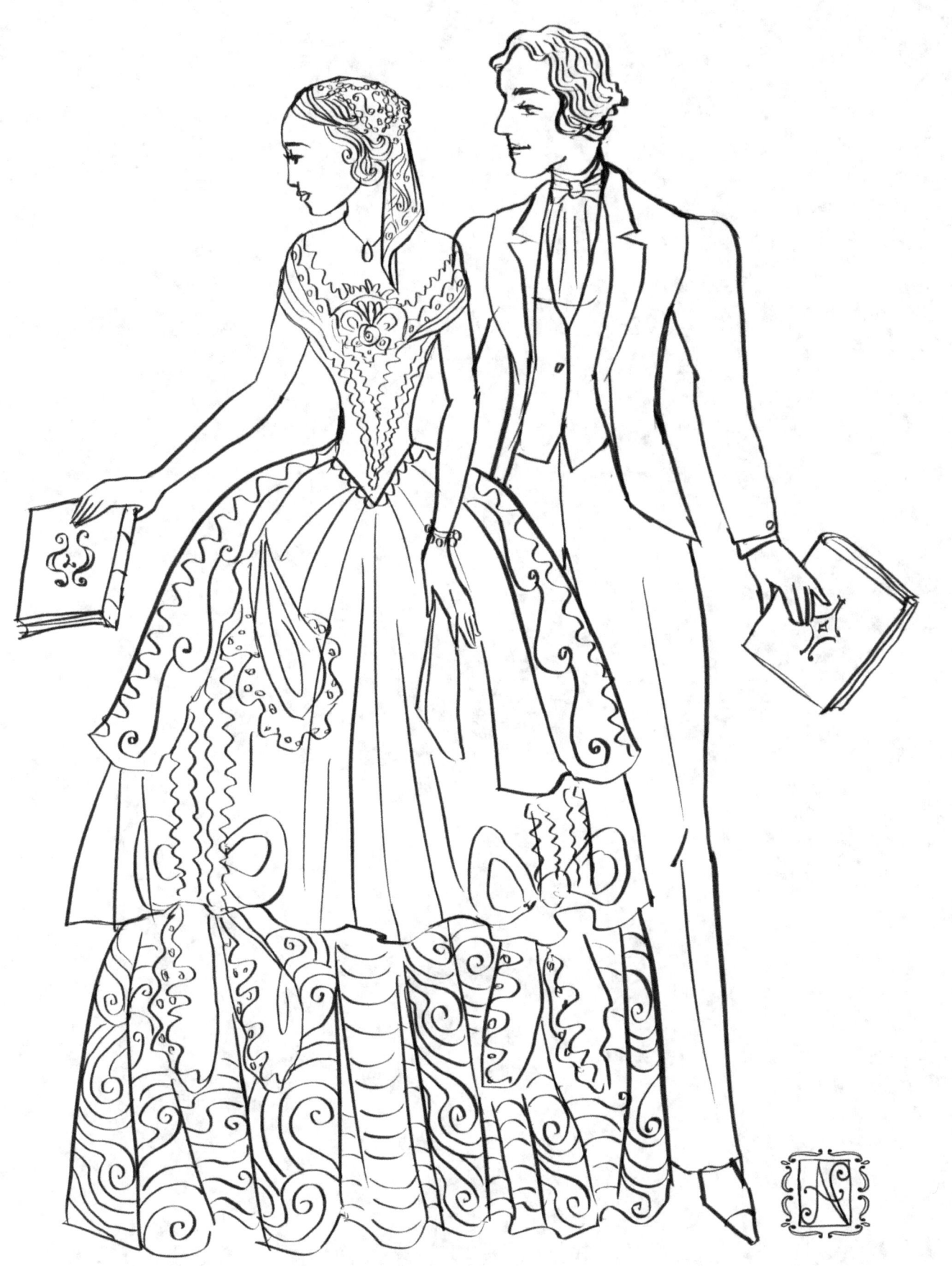

"I declare after all there is no enjoyment like reading!"

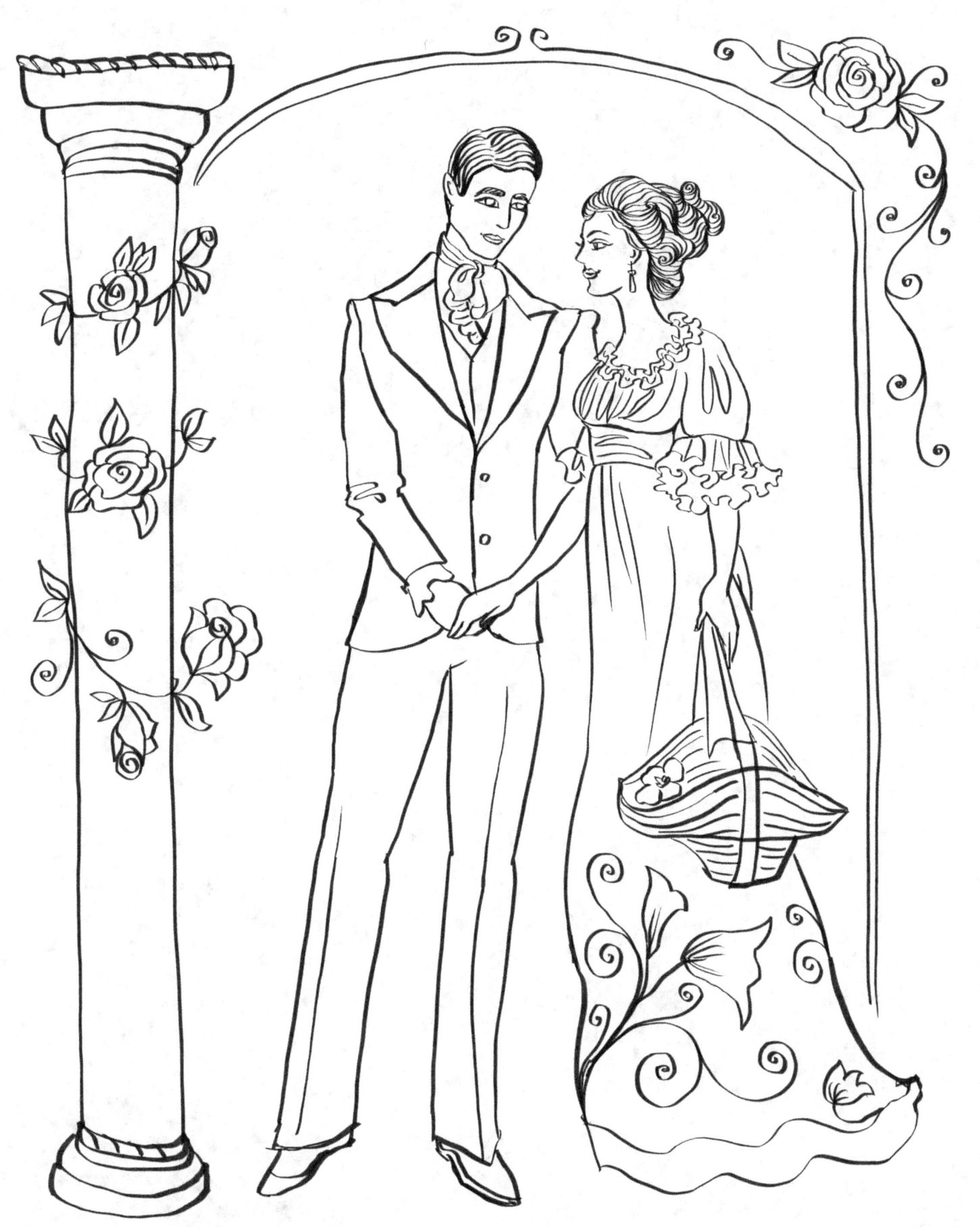

"*Think only of the past as its remembrance gives you pleasure.*"

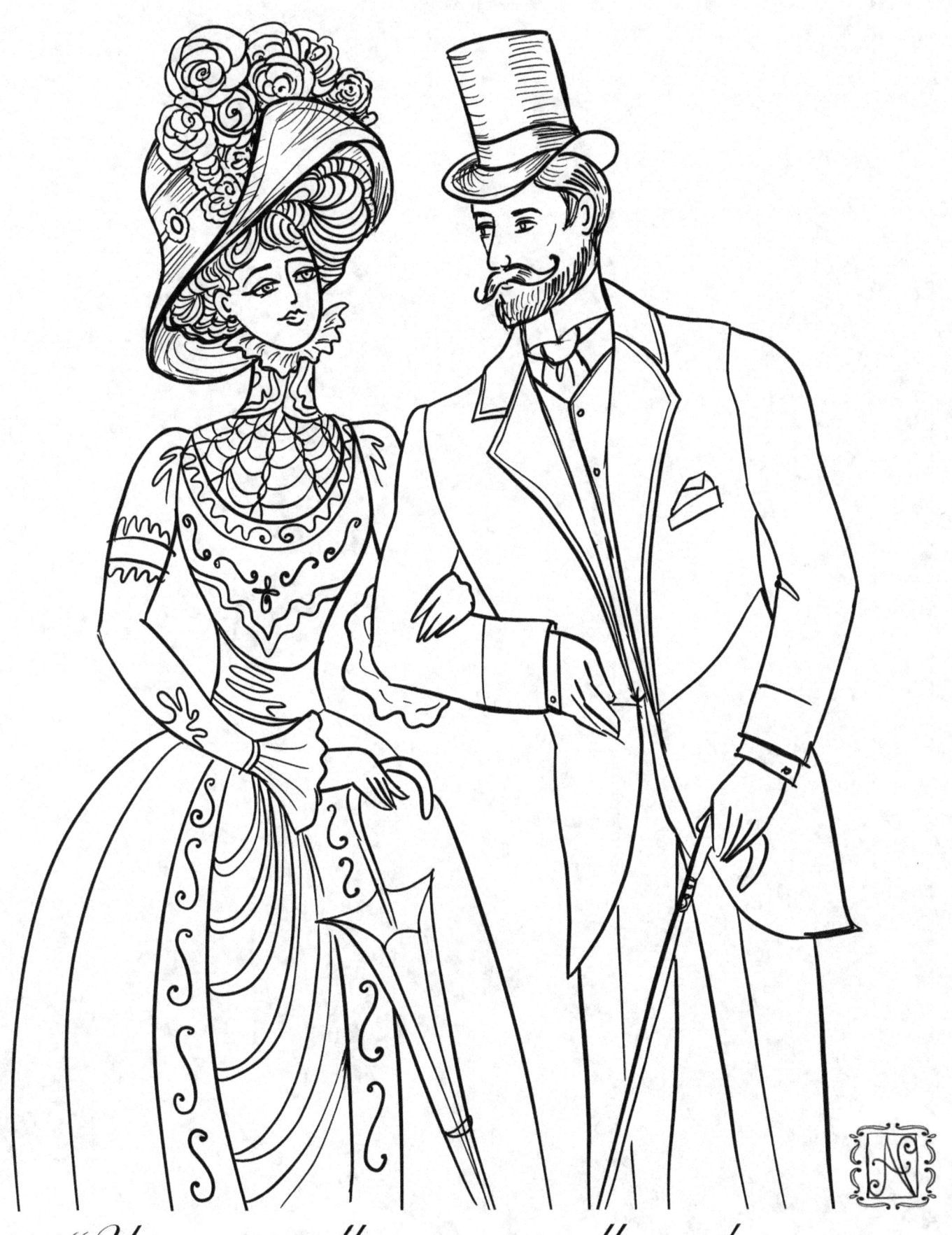

"You must allow me to tell you how ardently I admire and love you."

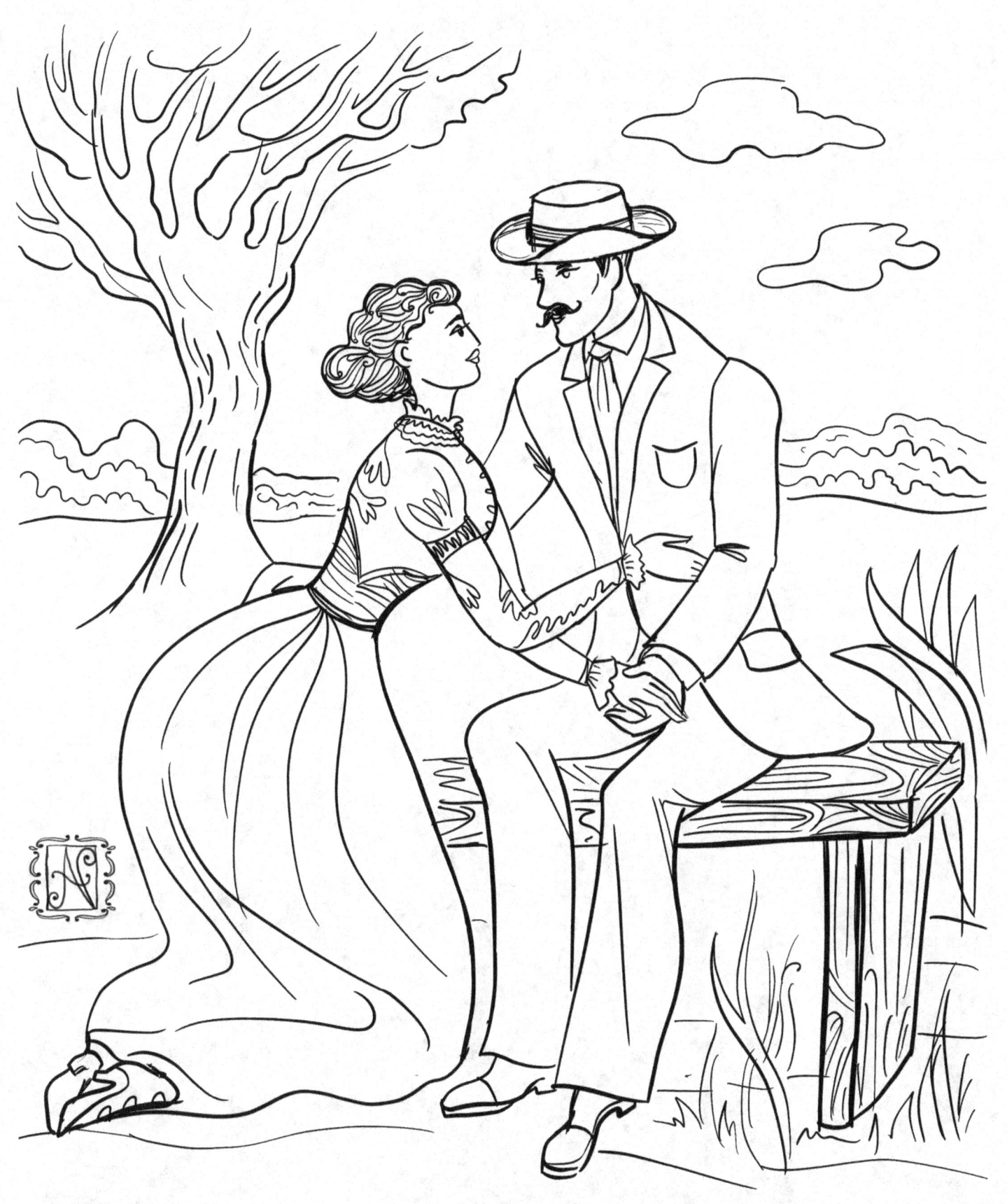

"Till this moment I never knew myself."

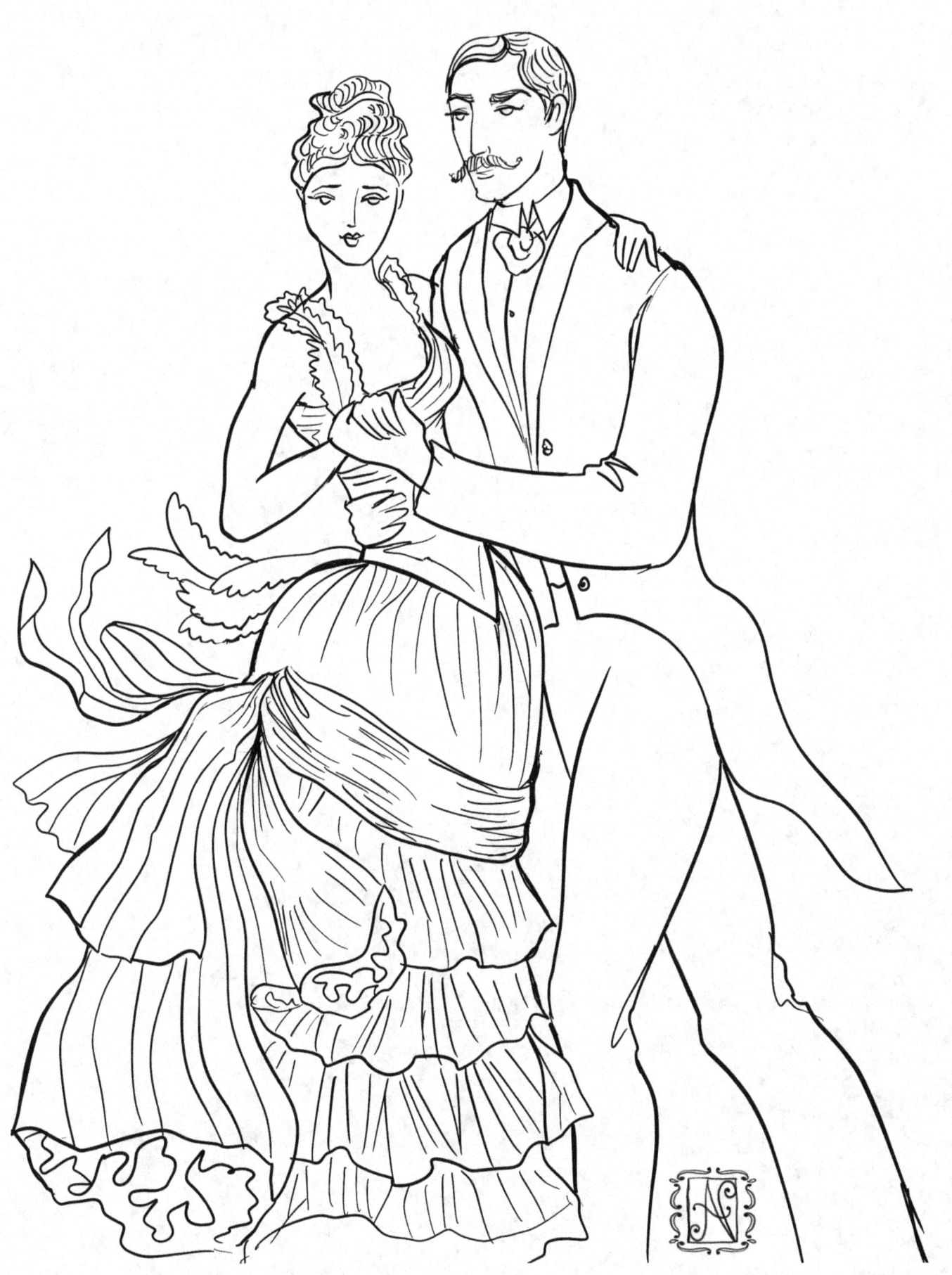

"*To be fond of dancing was a certain step towards falling in love.*"

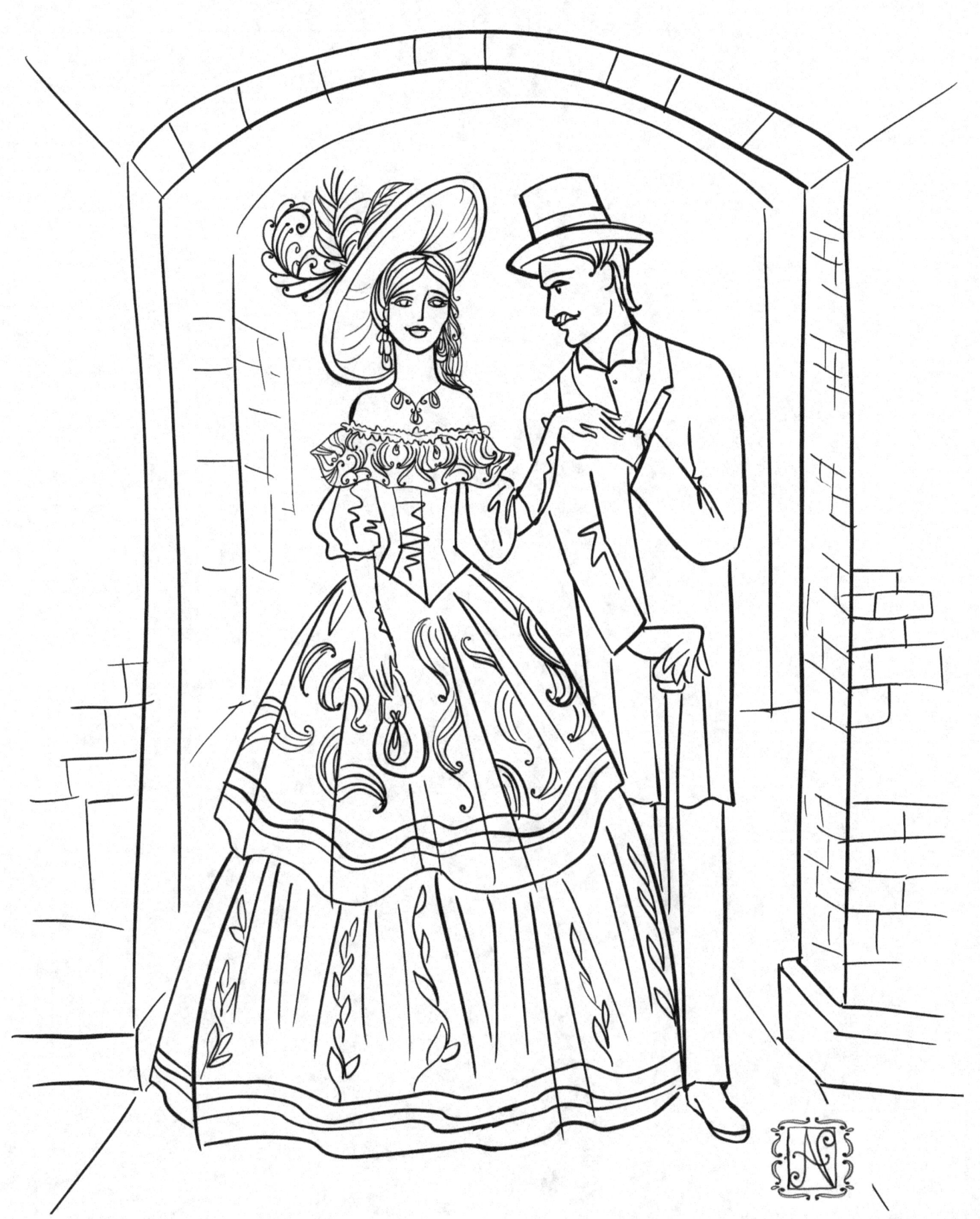

"I must learn to be content with being happier than I deserve."

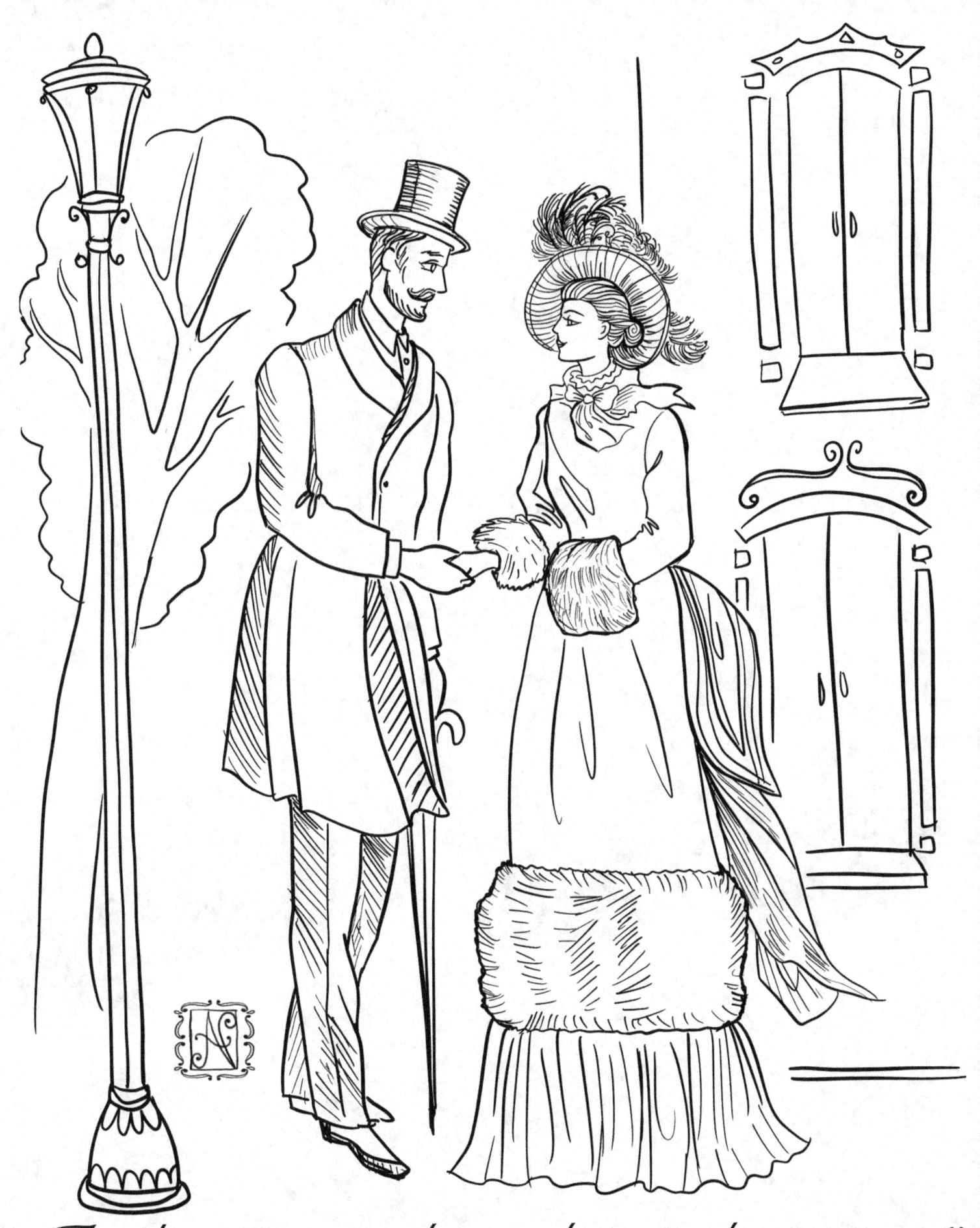
"The distance is nothing when one has motive."

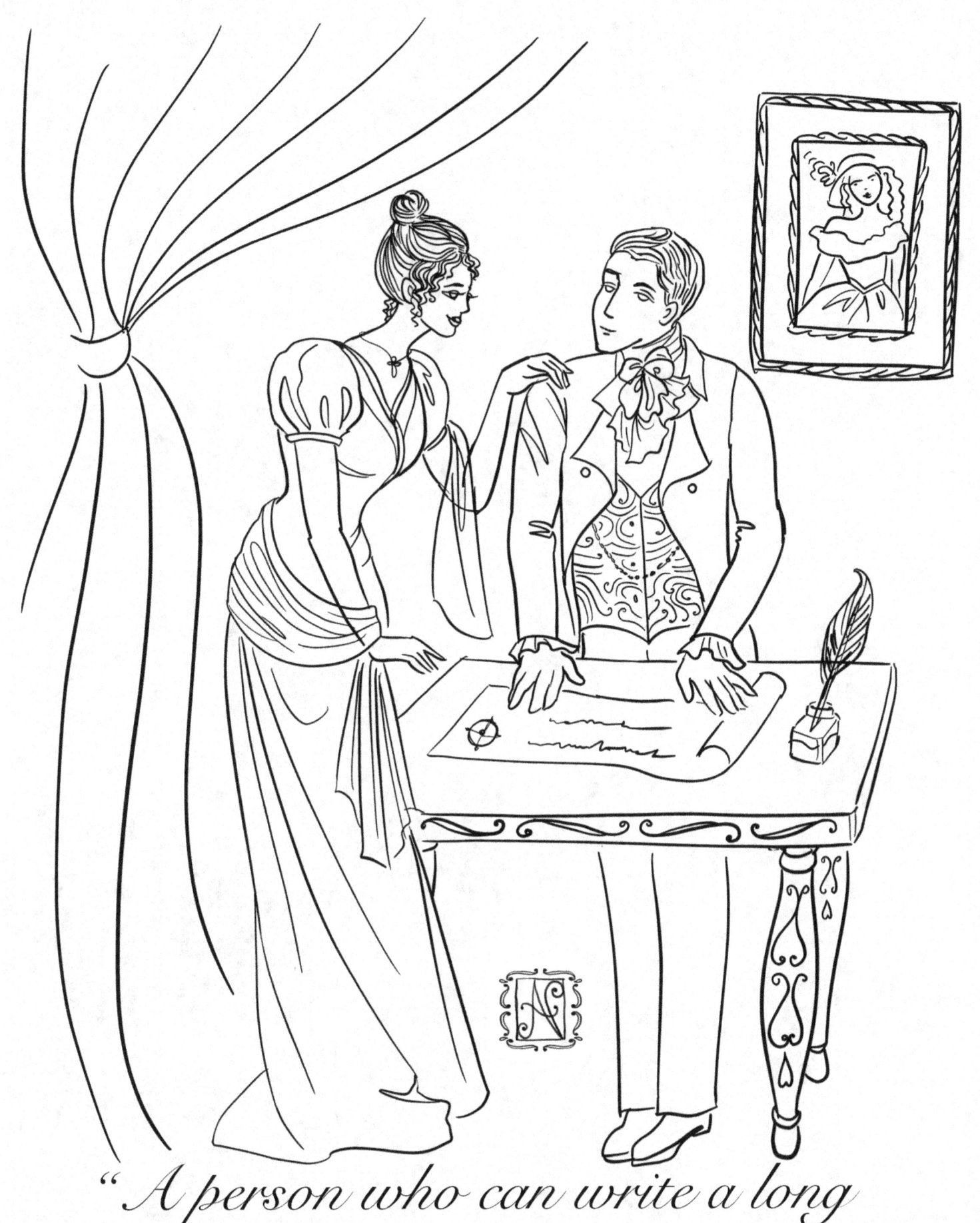

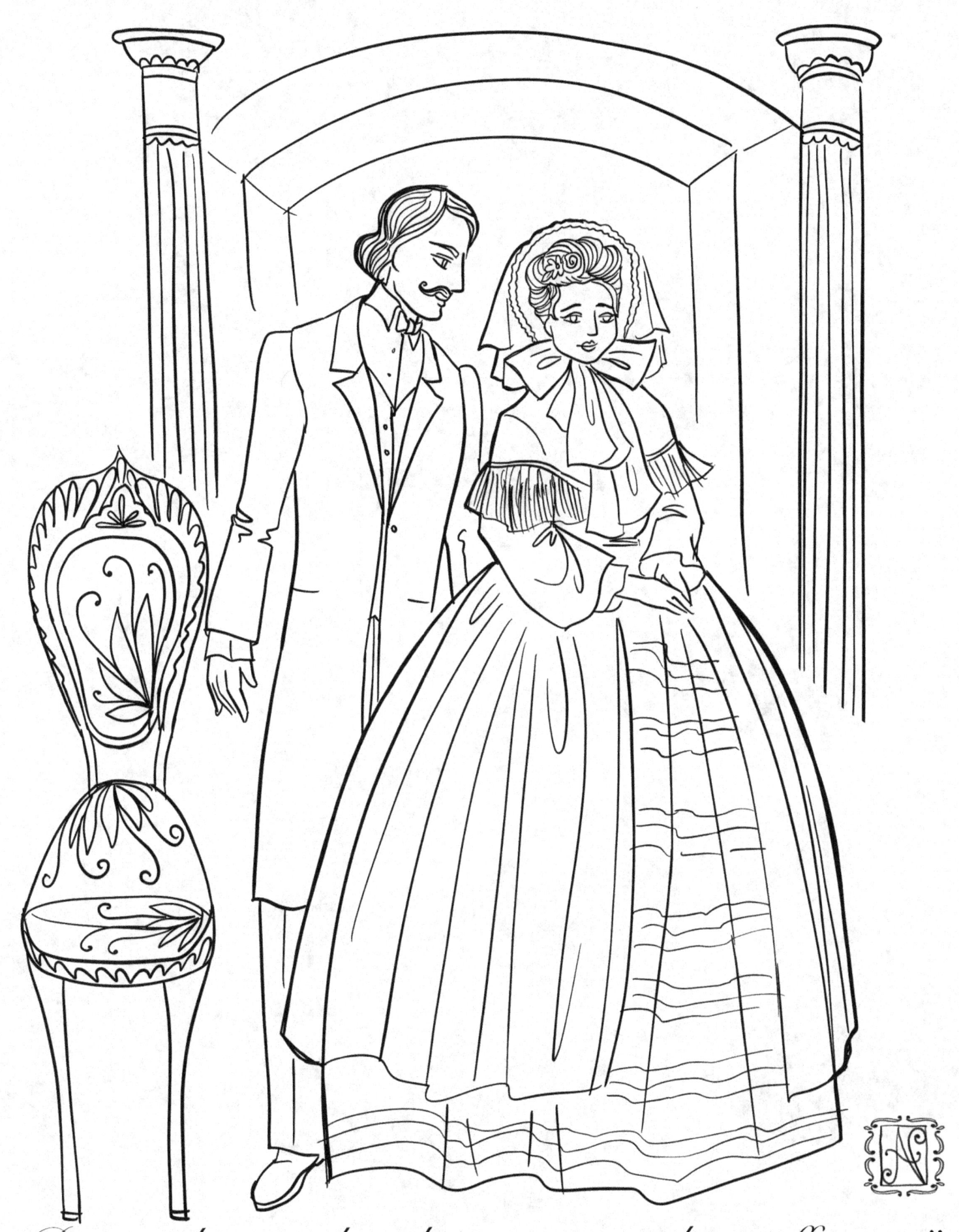
"Do anything rather than marry without affection."

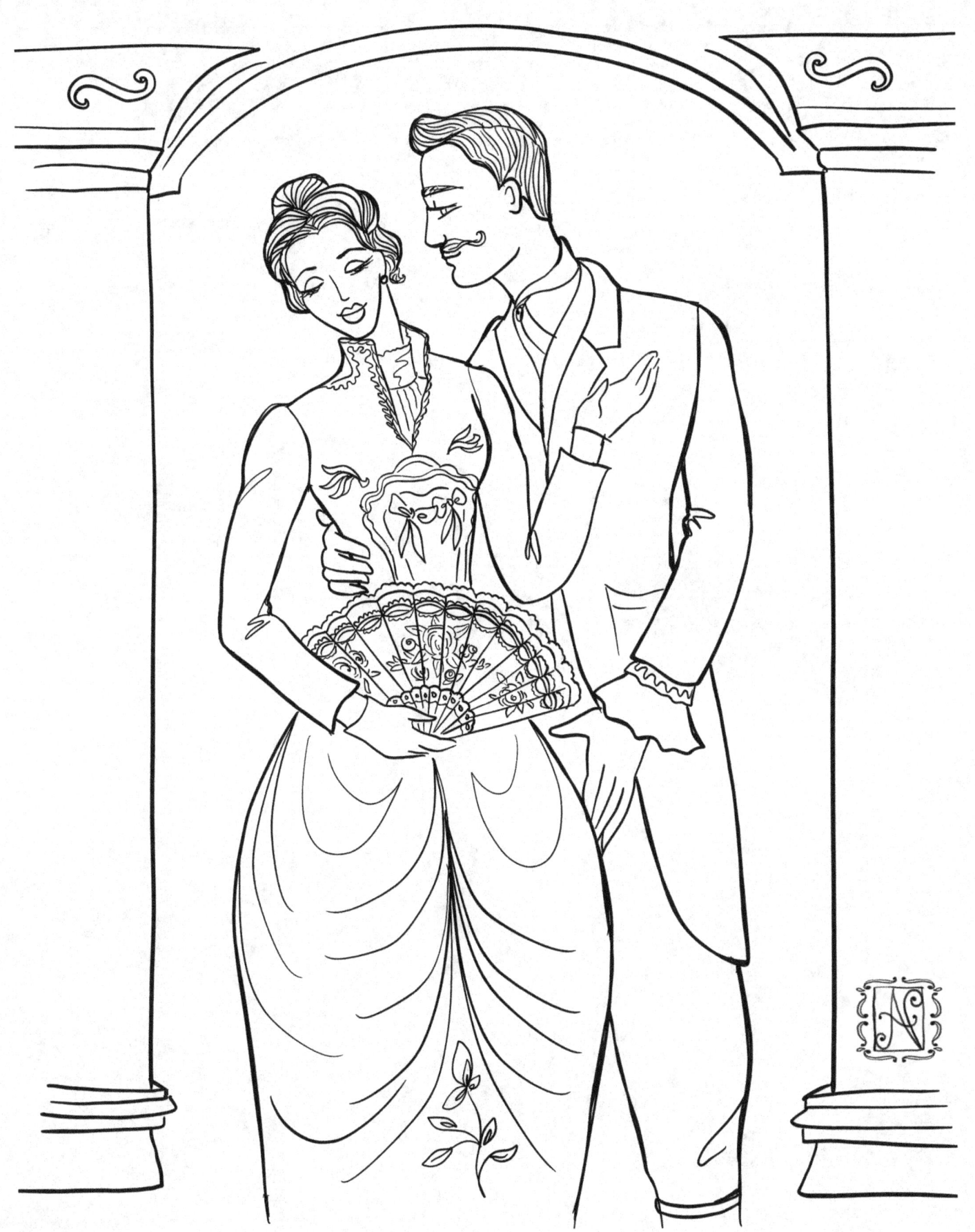

"*Nobody minds having what is too good for them.*"

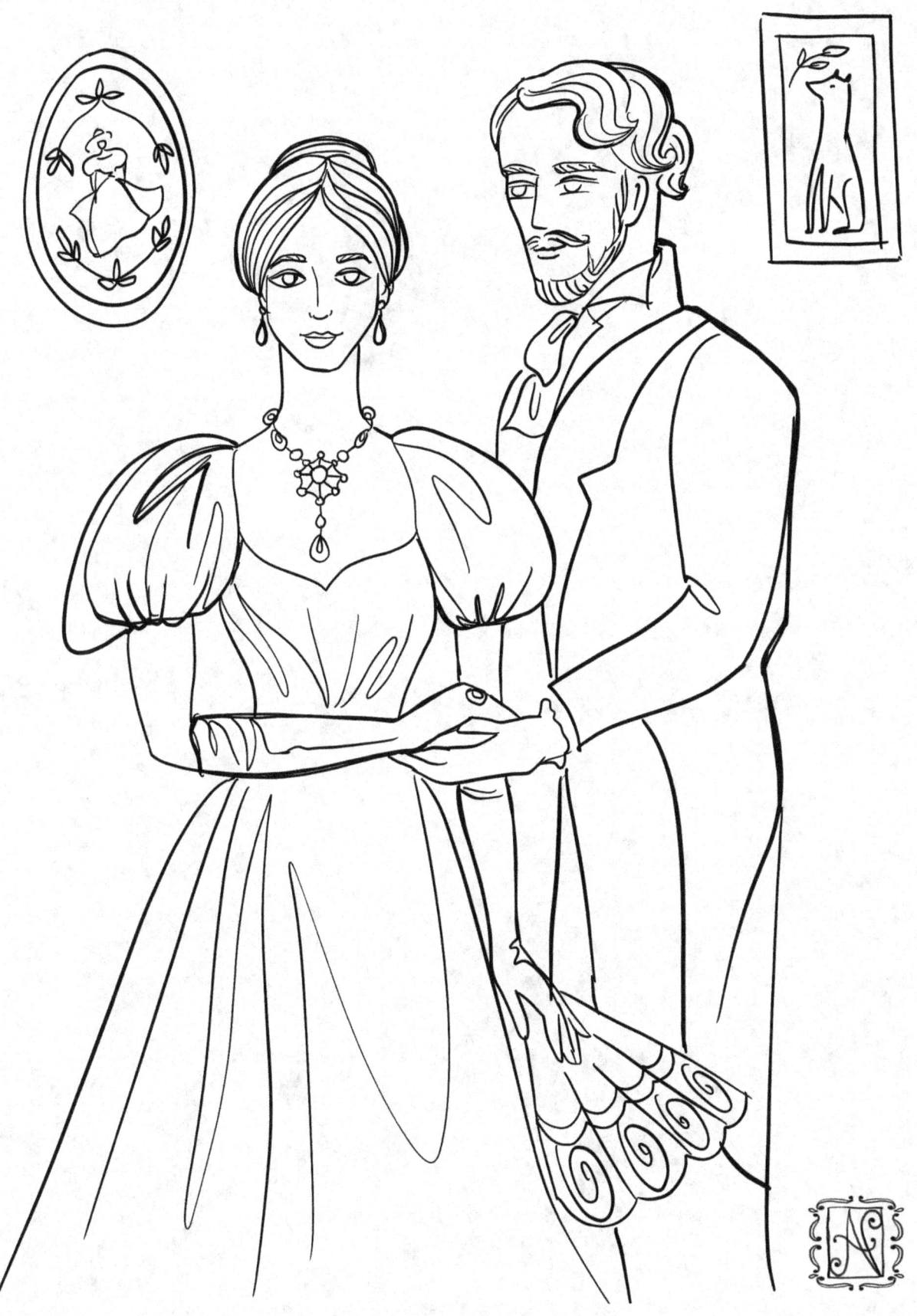

"If I loved you less, I might be able to talk about it more."

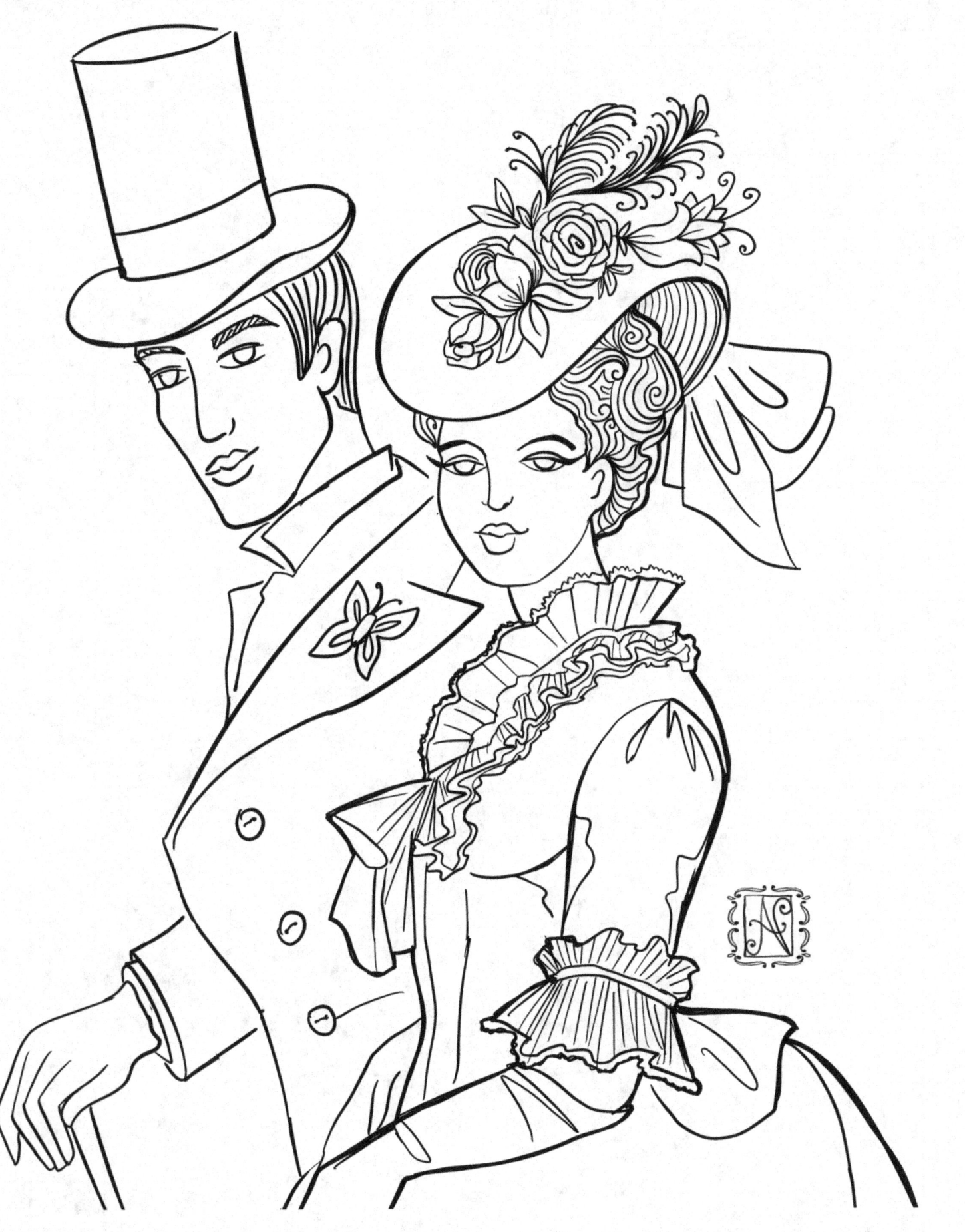
"Indulge your imagination in every possible flight."

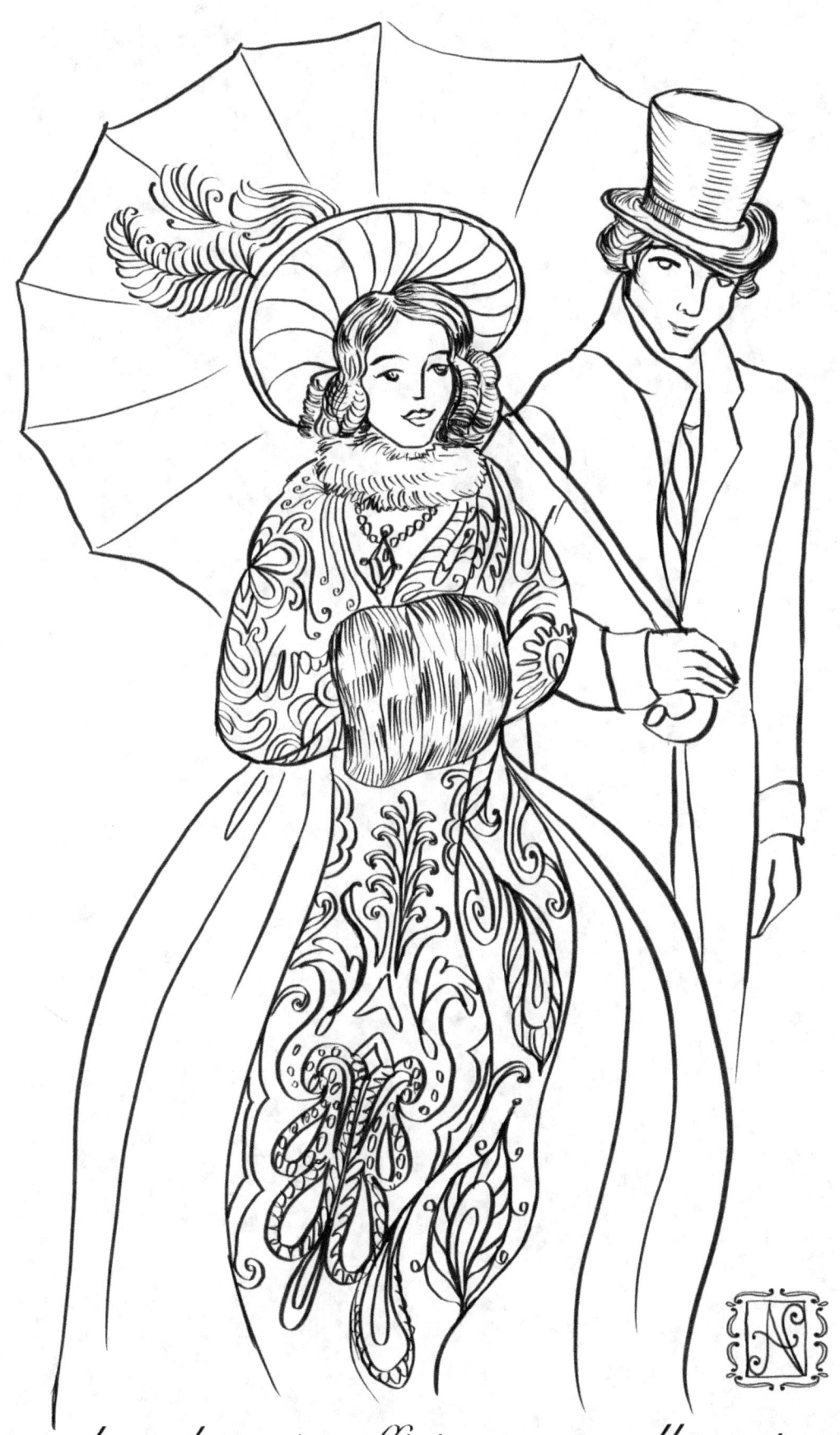

"You showed me how insufficient were all my pretensions to please a woman worthy of being pleased."

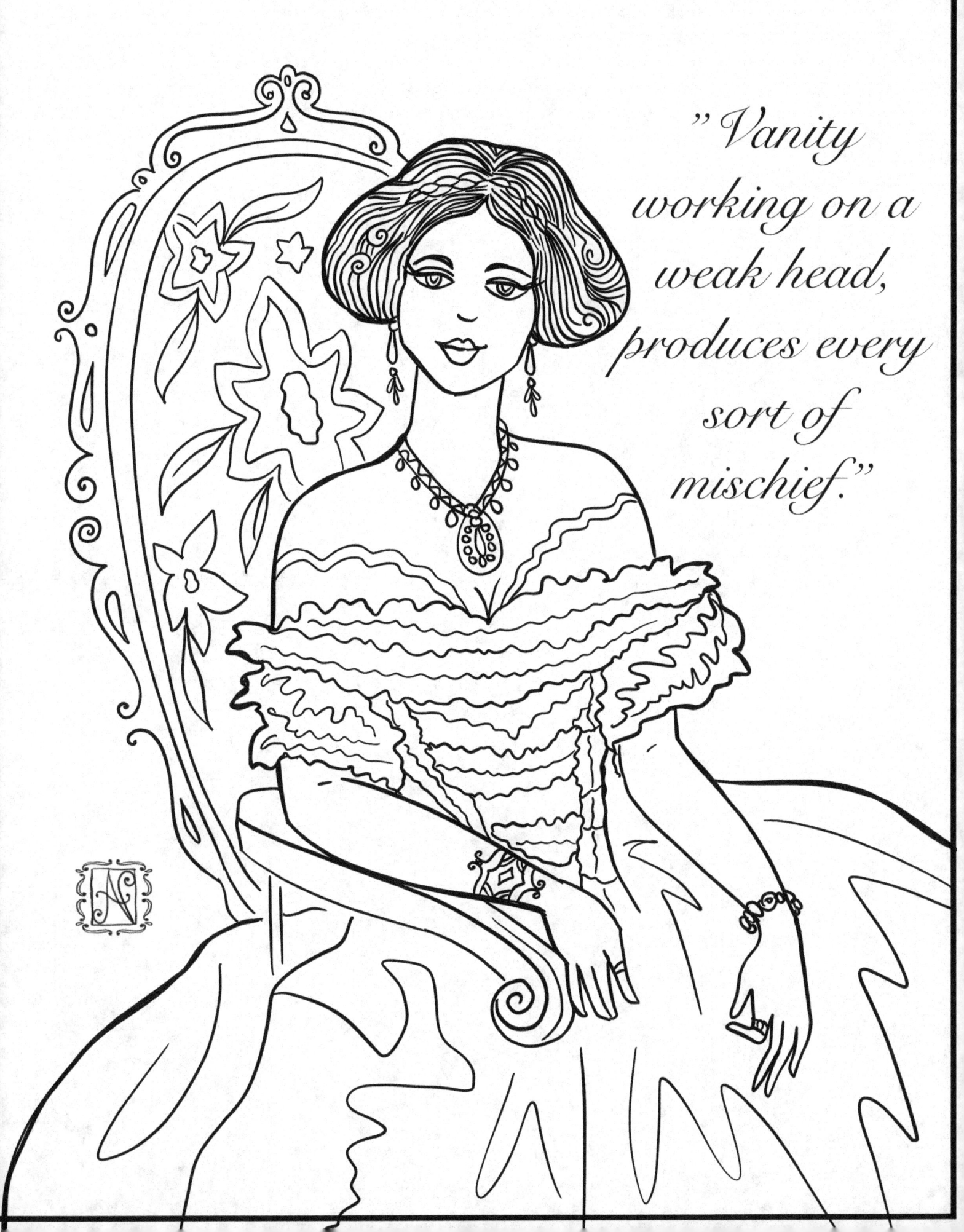

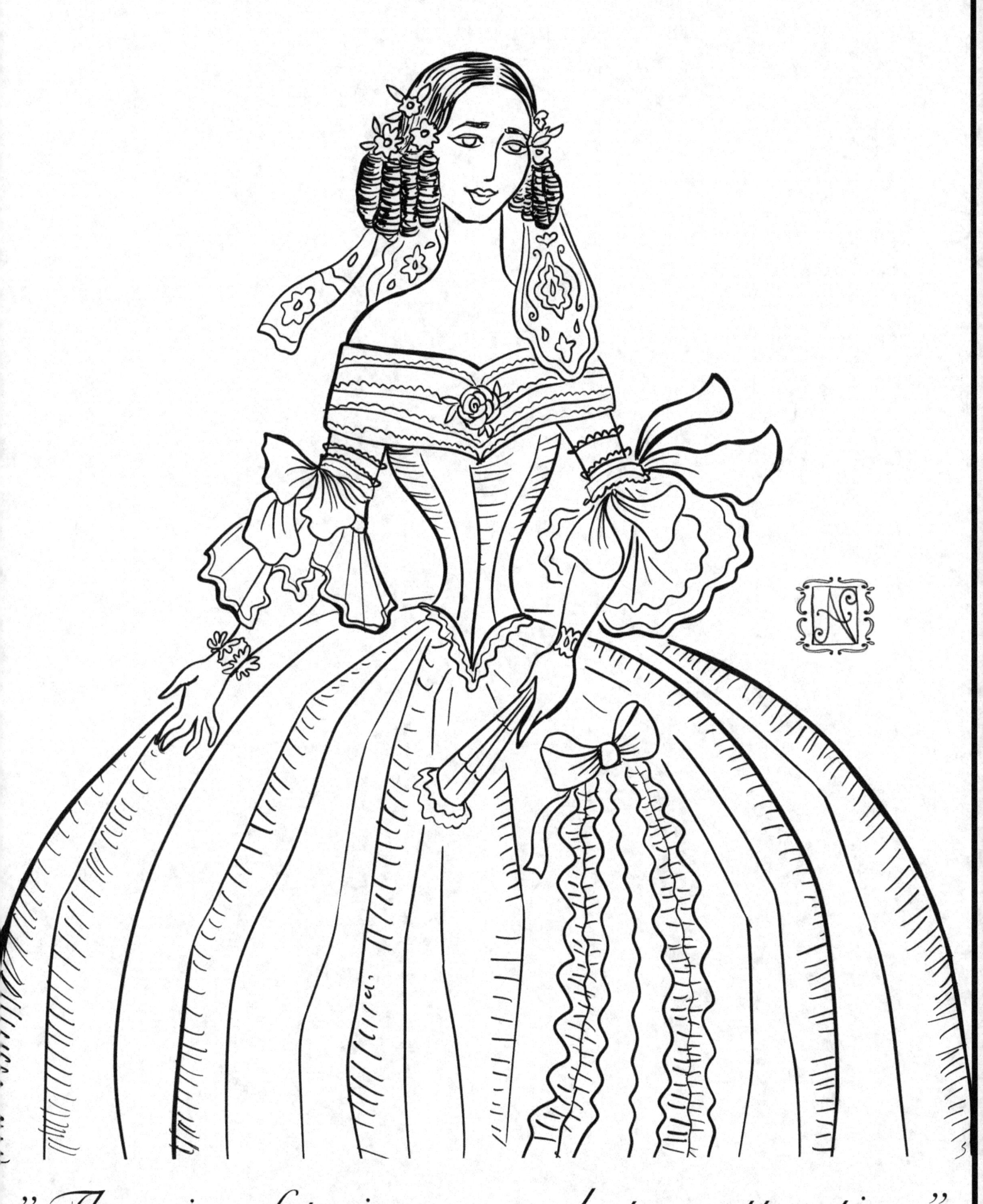

"There is safety in reserve, but no attraction."

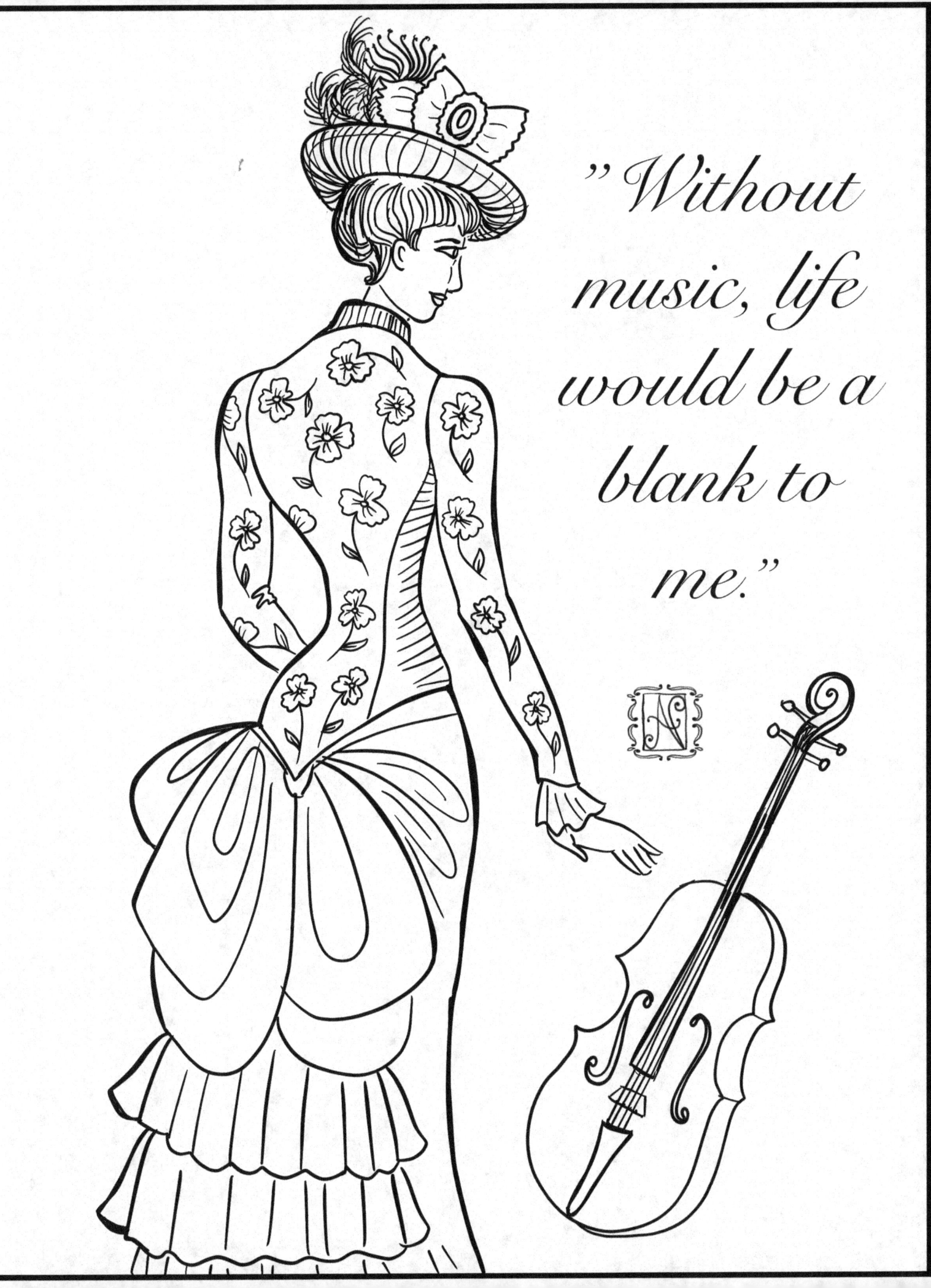

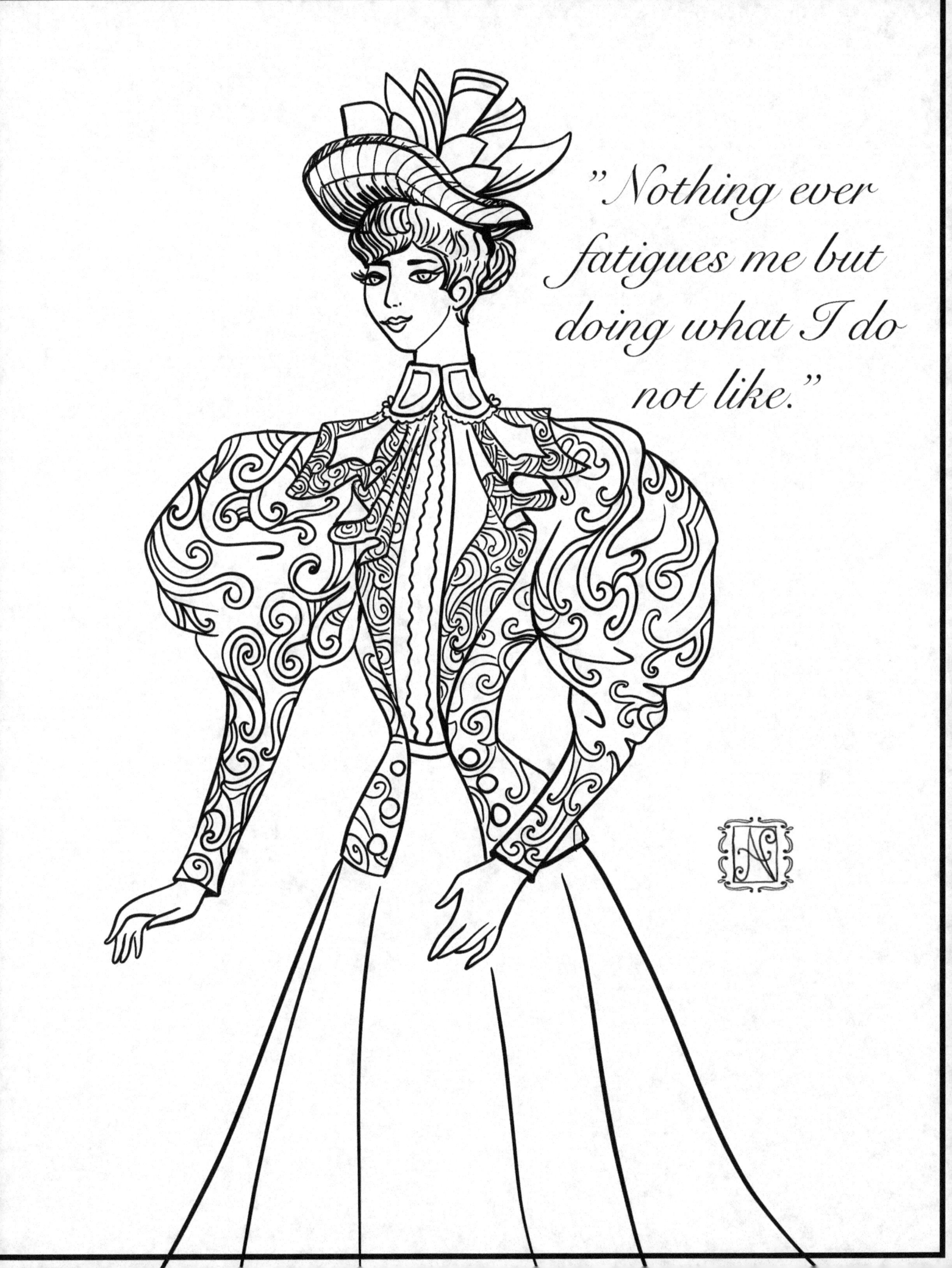

"Nothing ever fatigues me but doing what I do not like."

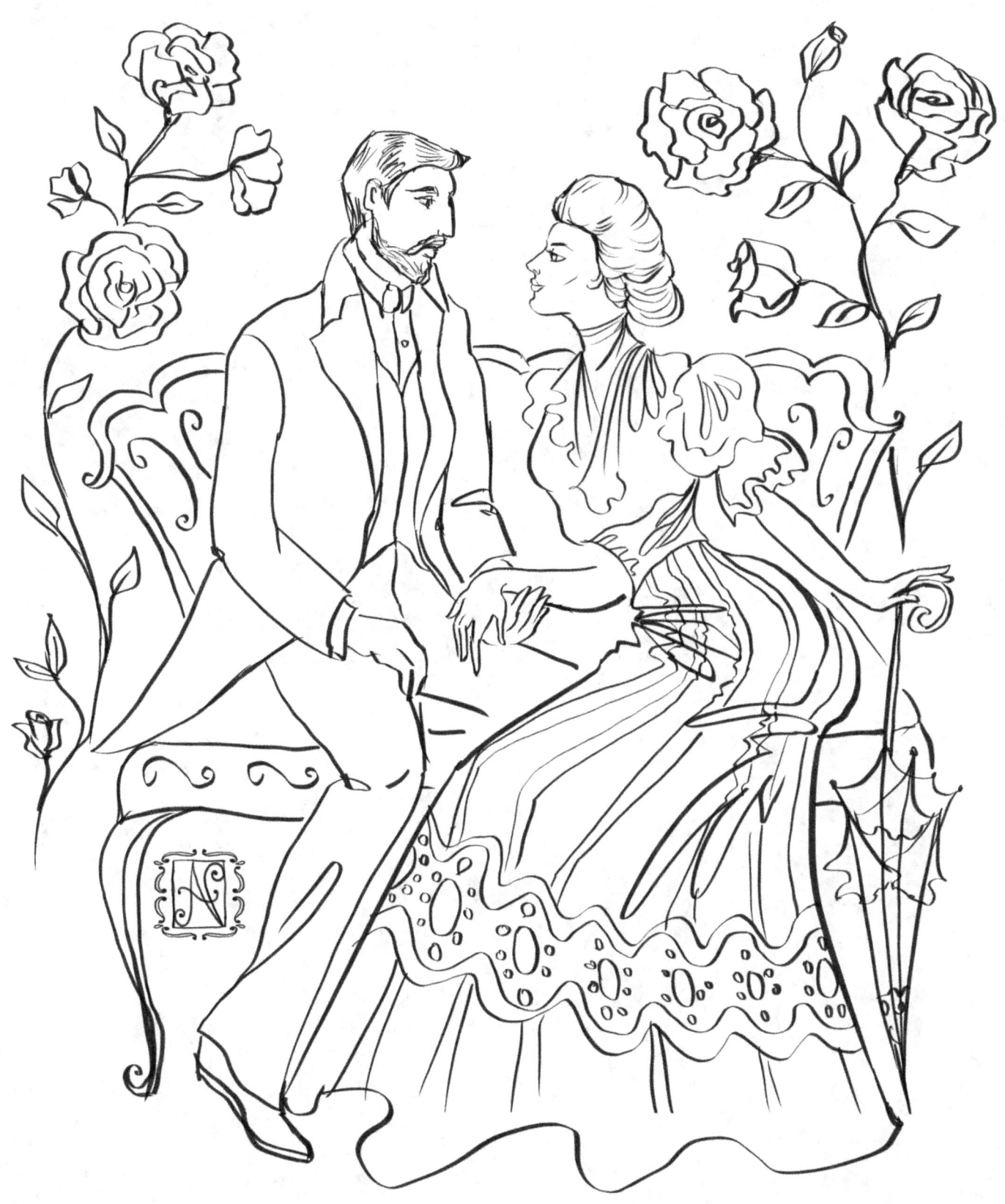

"It is happy for you that you possess the talent of flattering with delicacy."

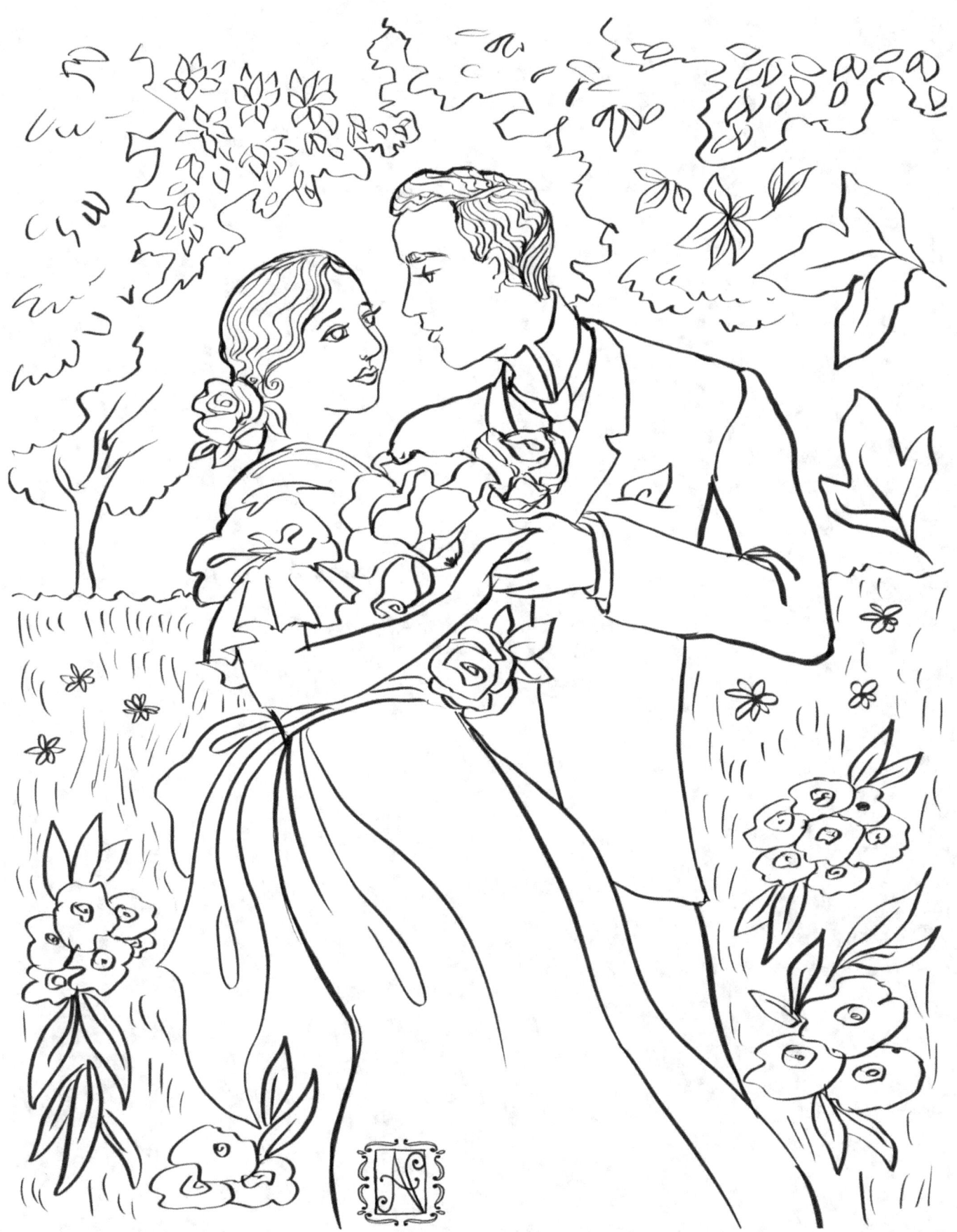

"Is not general incivility the very essence of love?"

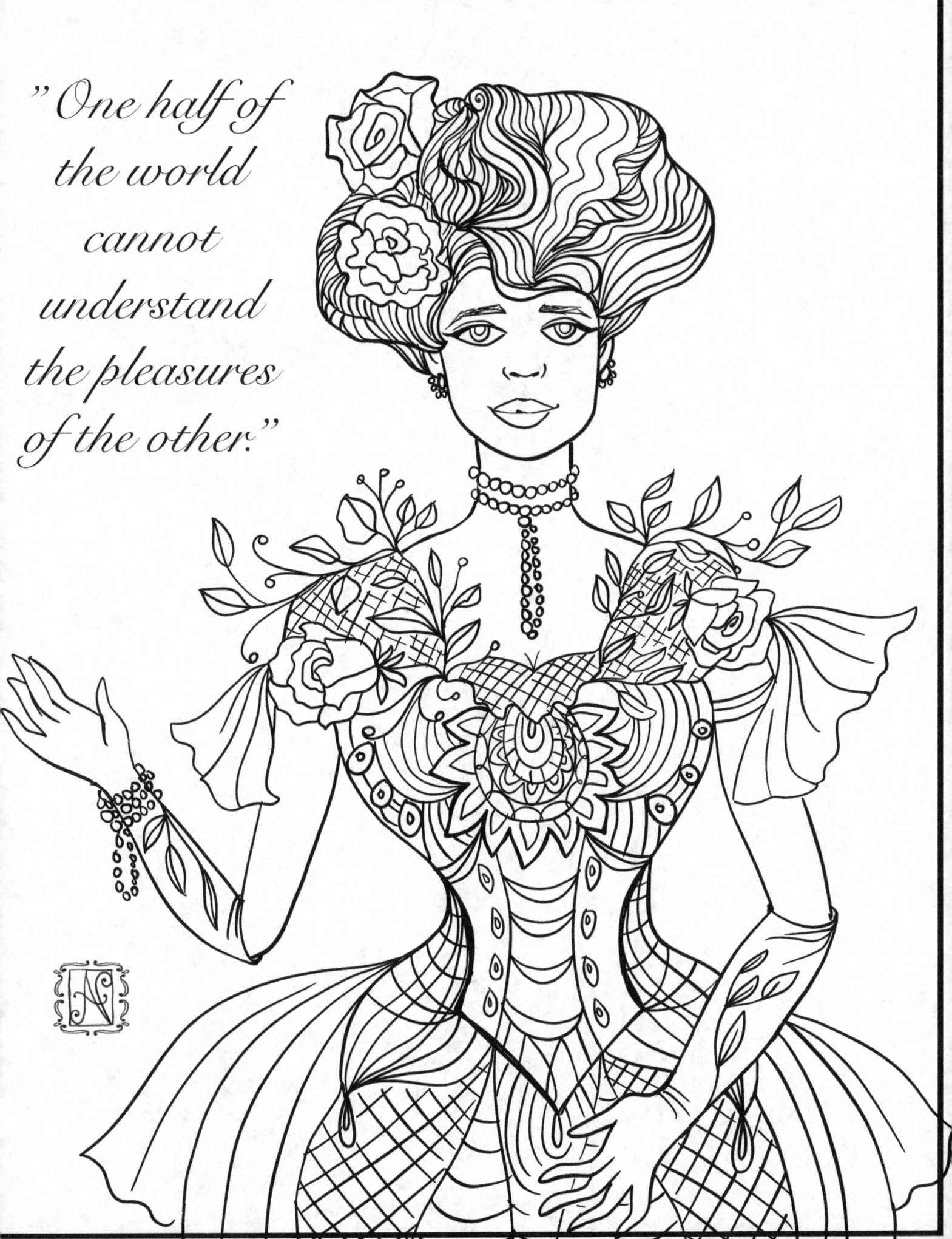

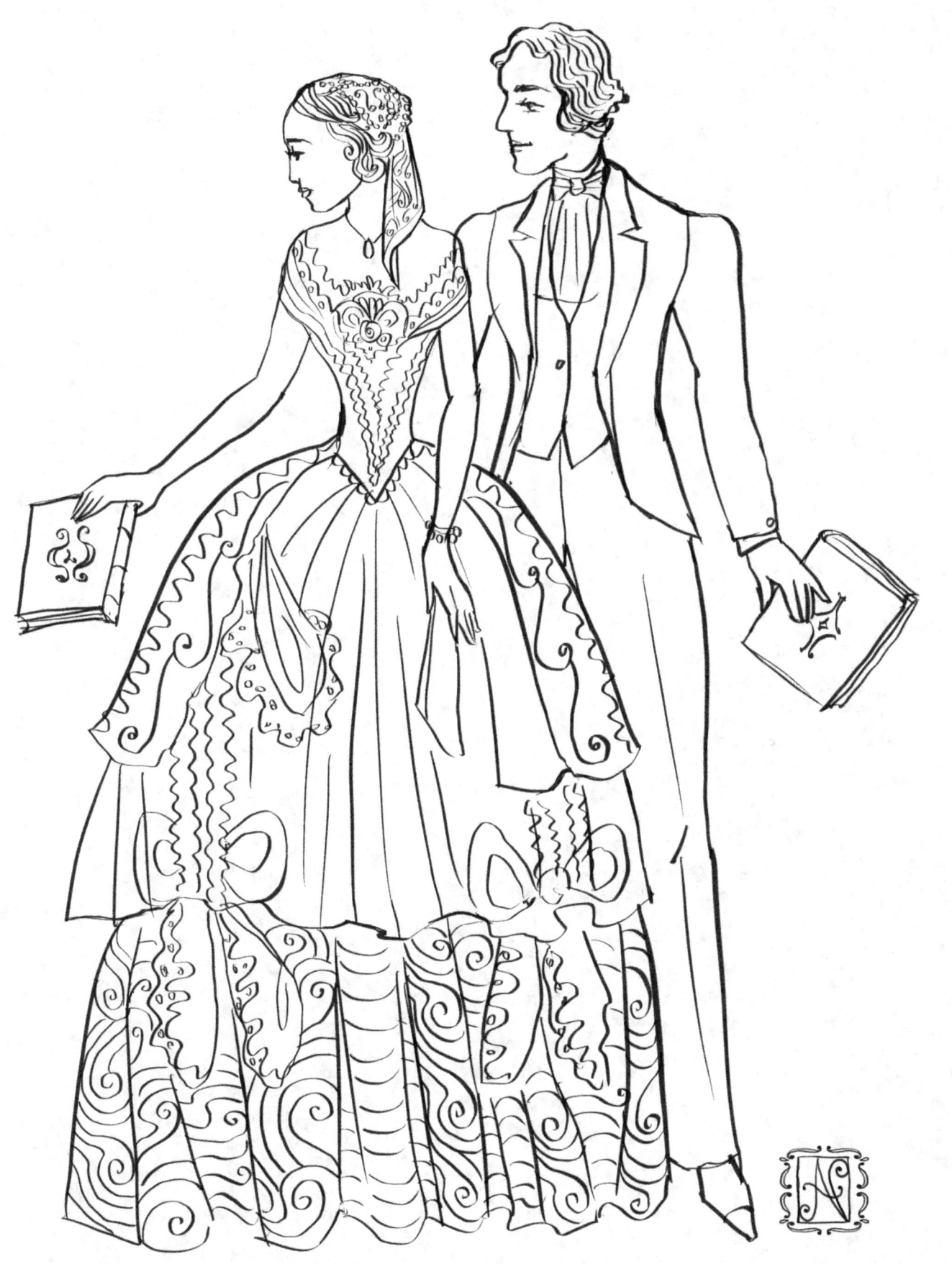

"I declare after all there is no enjoyment like reading!"

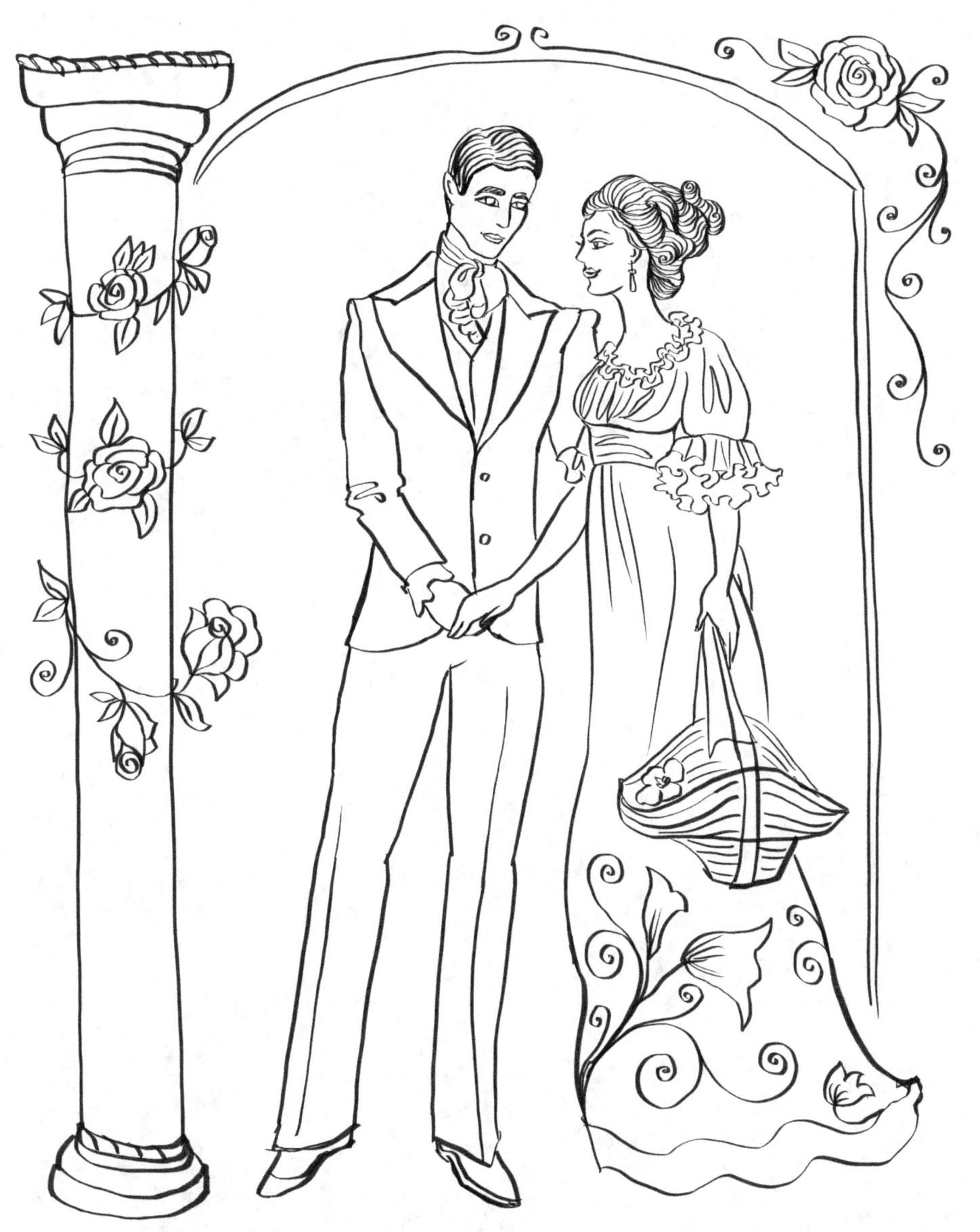

"Think only of the past as its remembrance gives you pleasure."

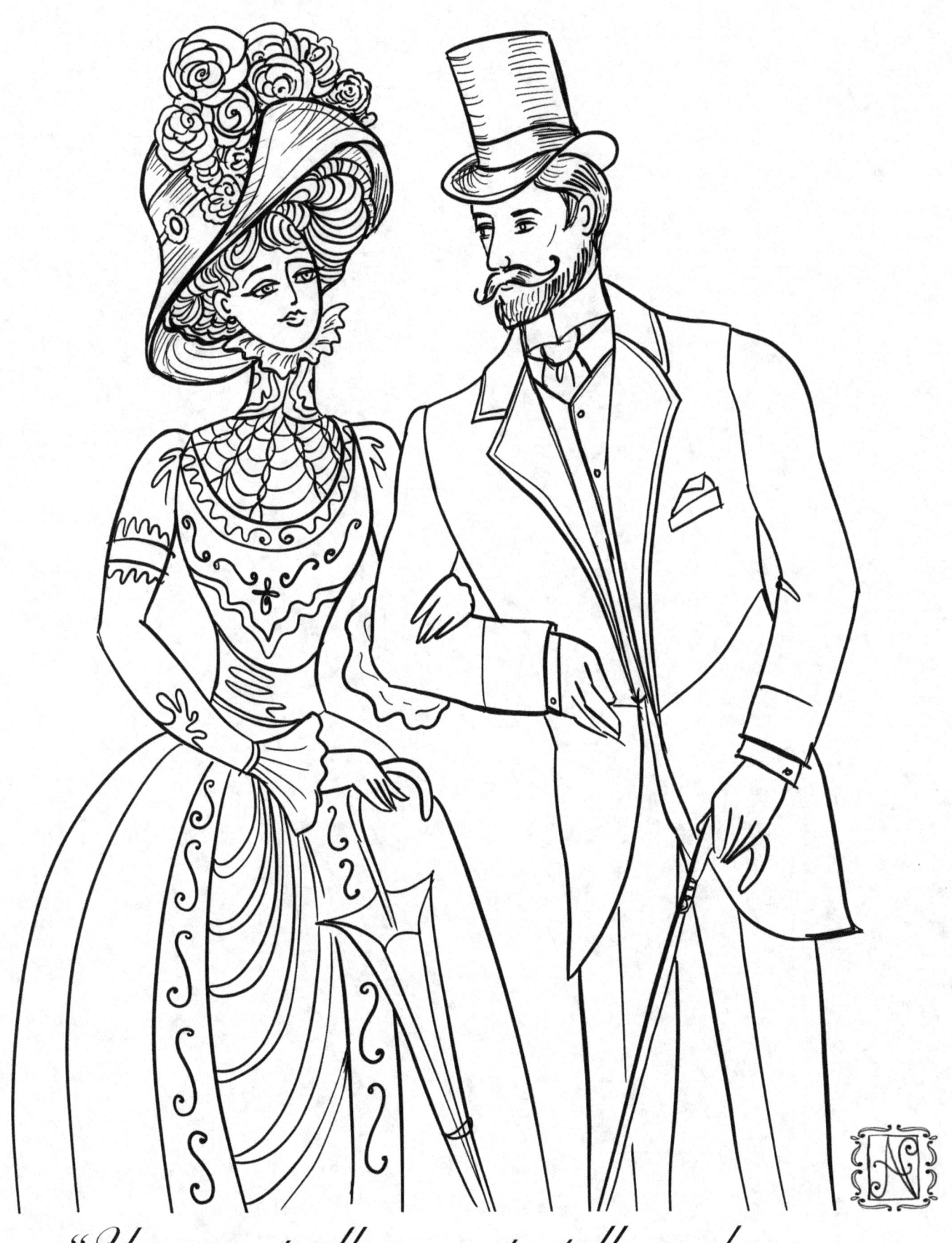

"*You must allow me to tell you how ardently I admire and love you.*"

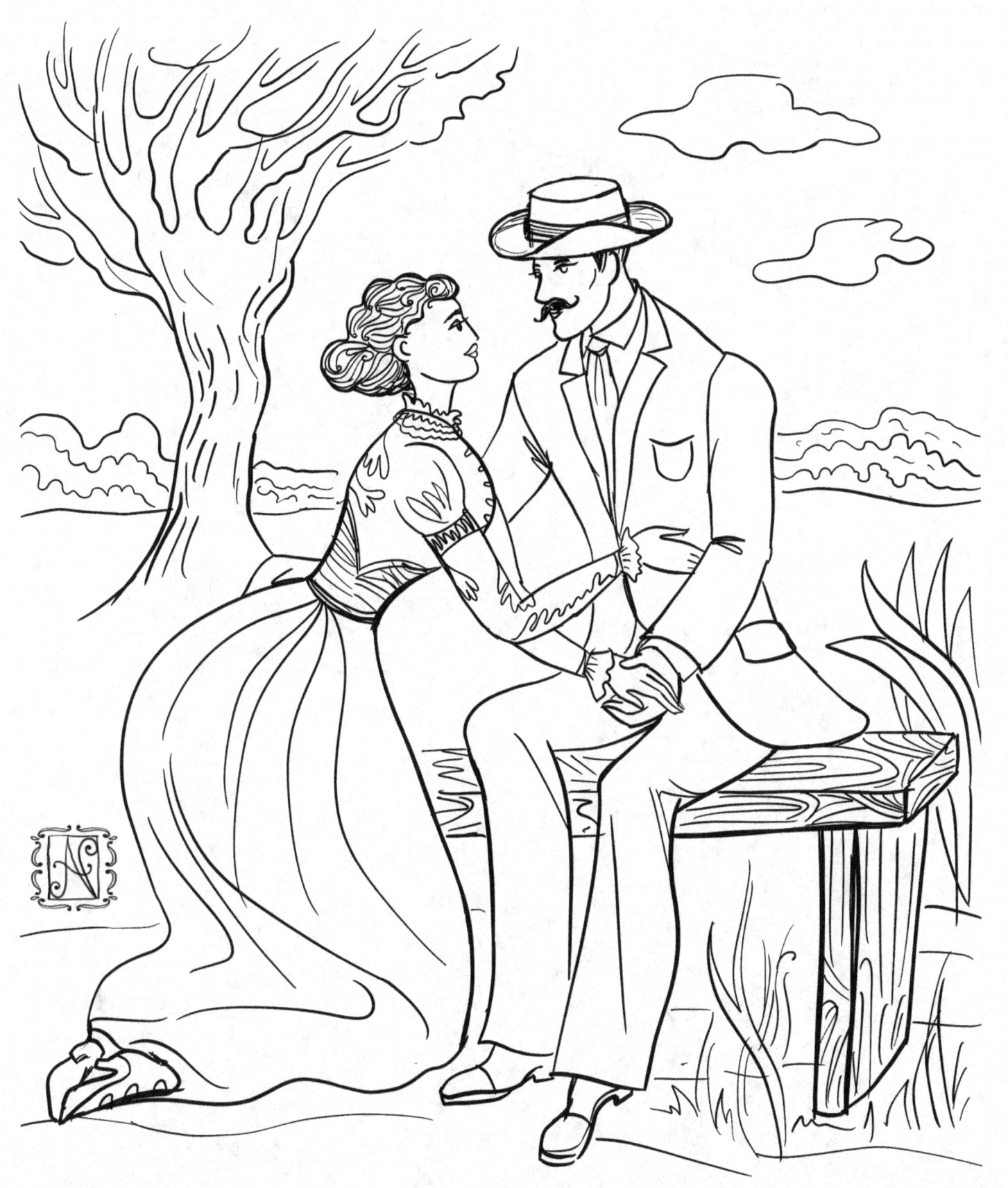

"Till this moment I never knew myself."

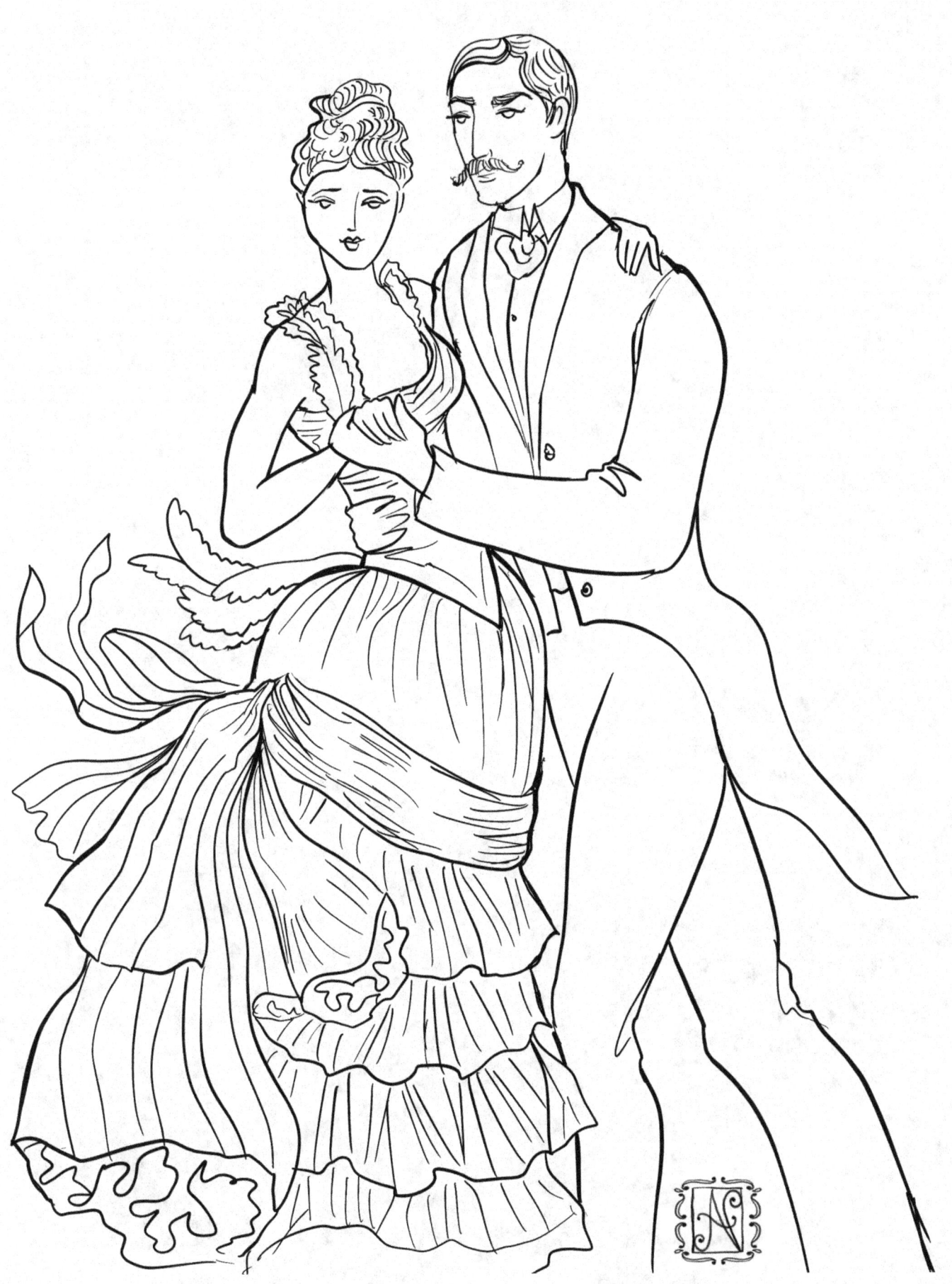

"To be fond of dancing was a certain step towards falling in love."

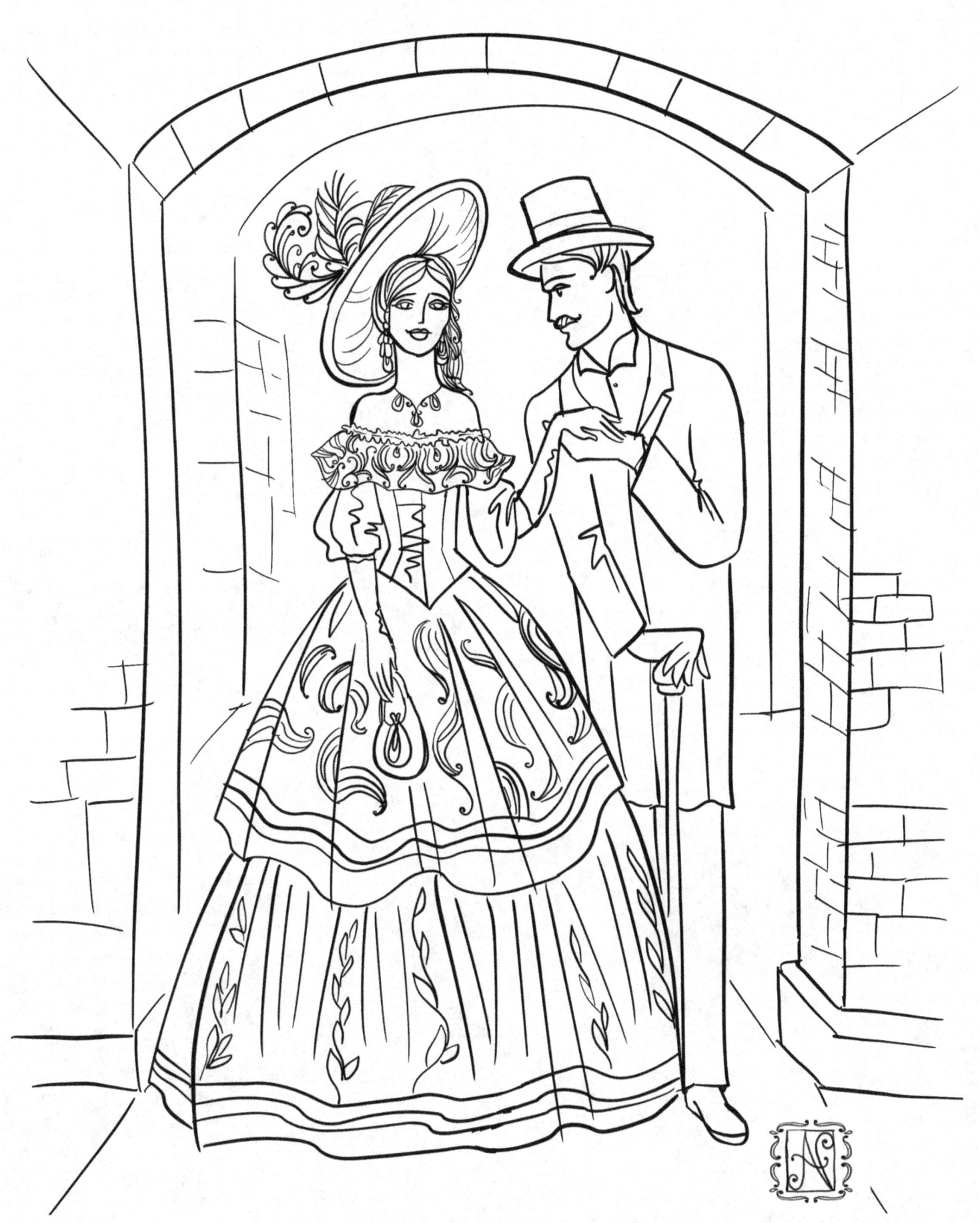

"I must learn to be content with being happier than I deserve."

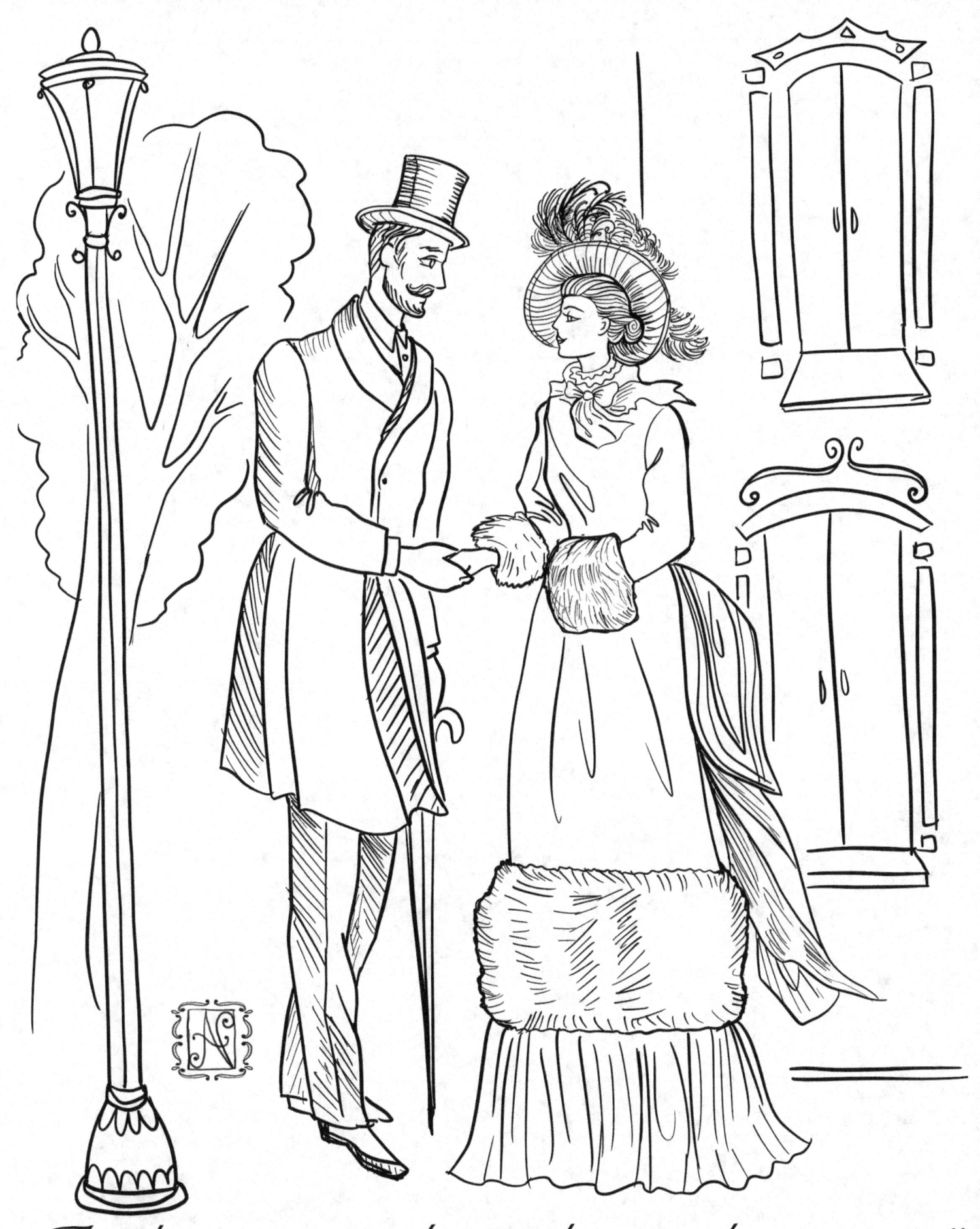
"The distance is nothing when one has motive."

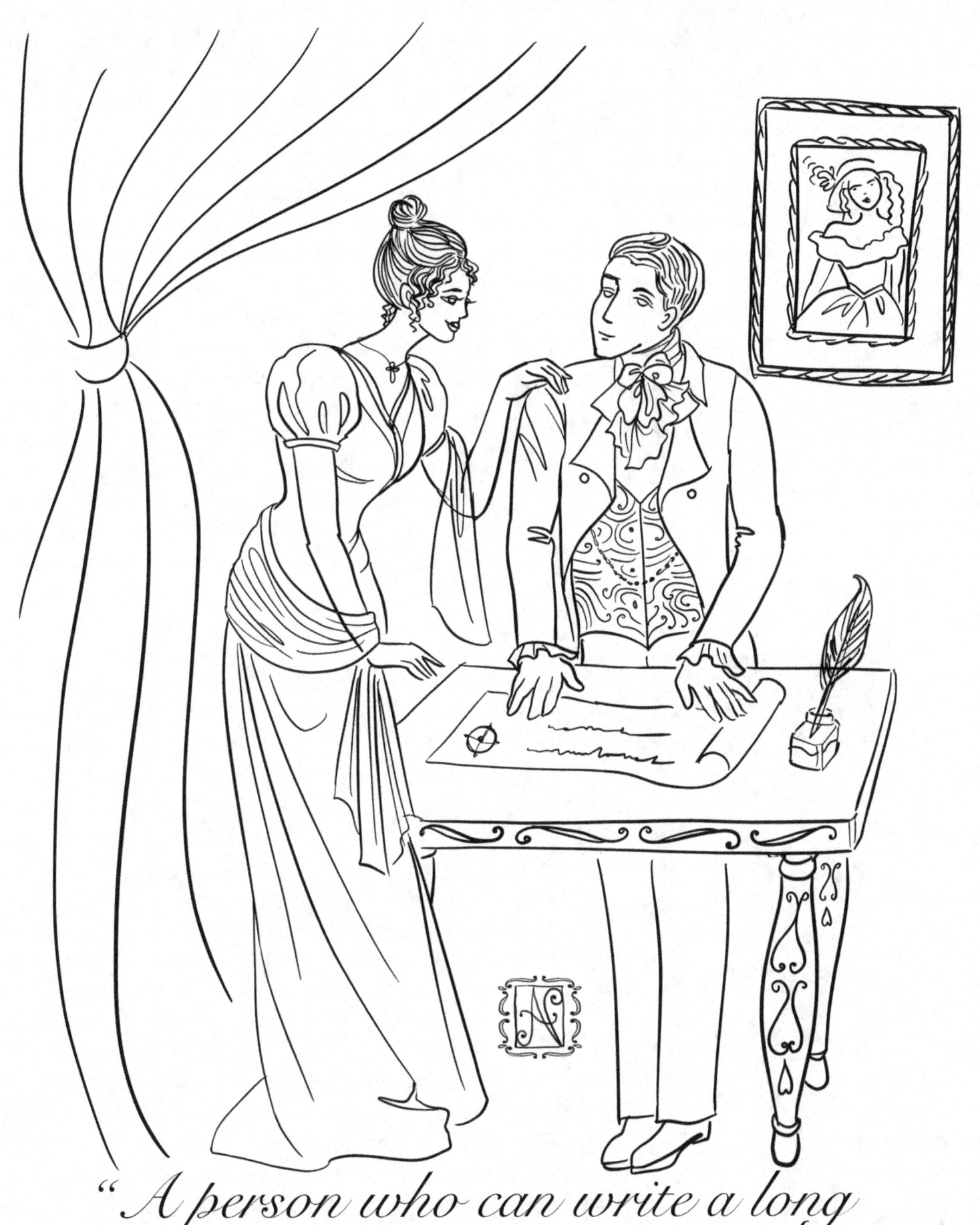

"A person who can write a long letter with ease, cannot write ill."

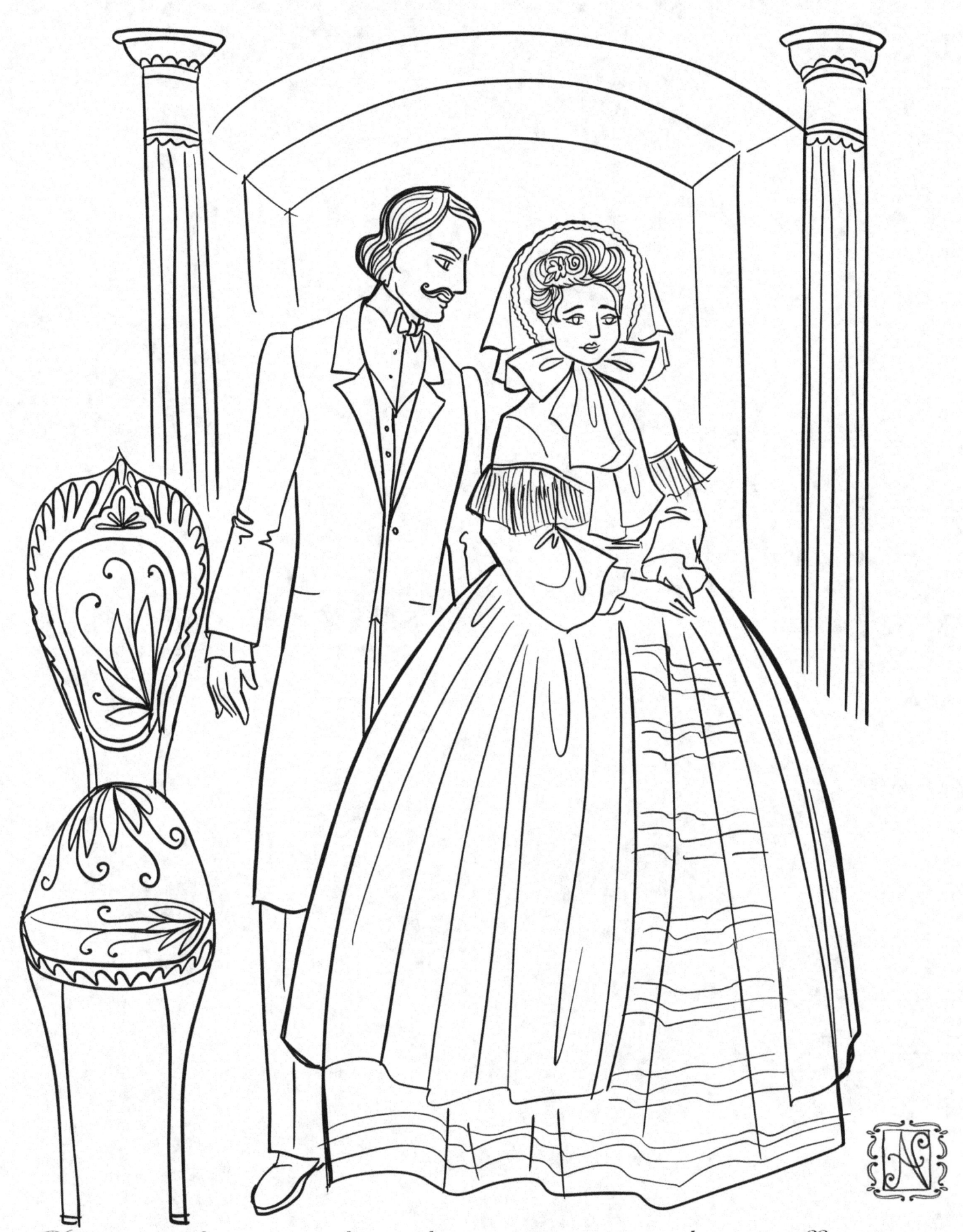

"Do anything rather than marry without affection."

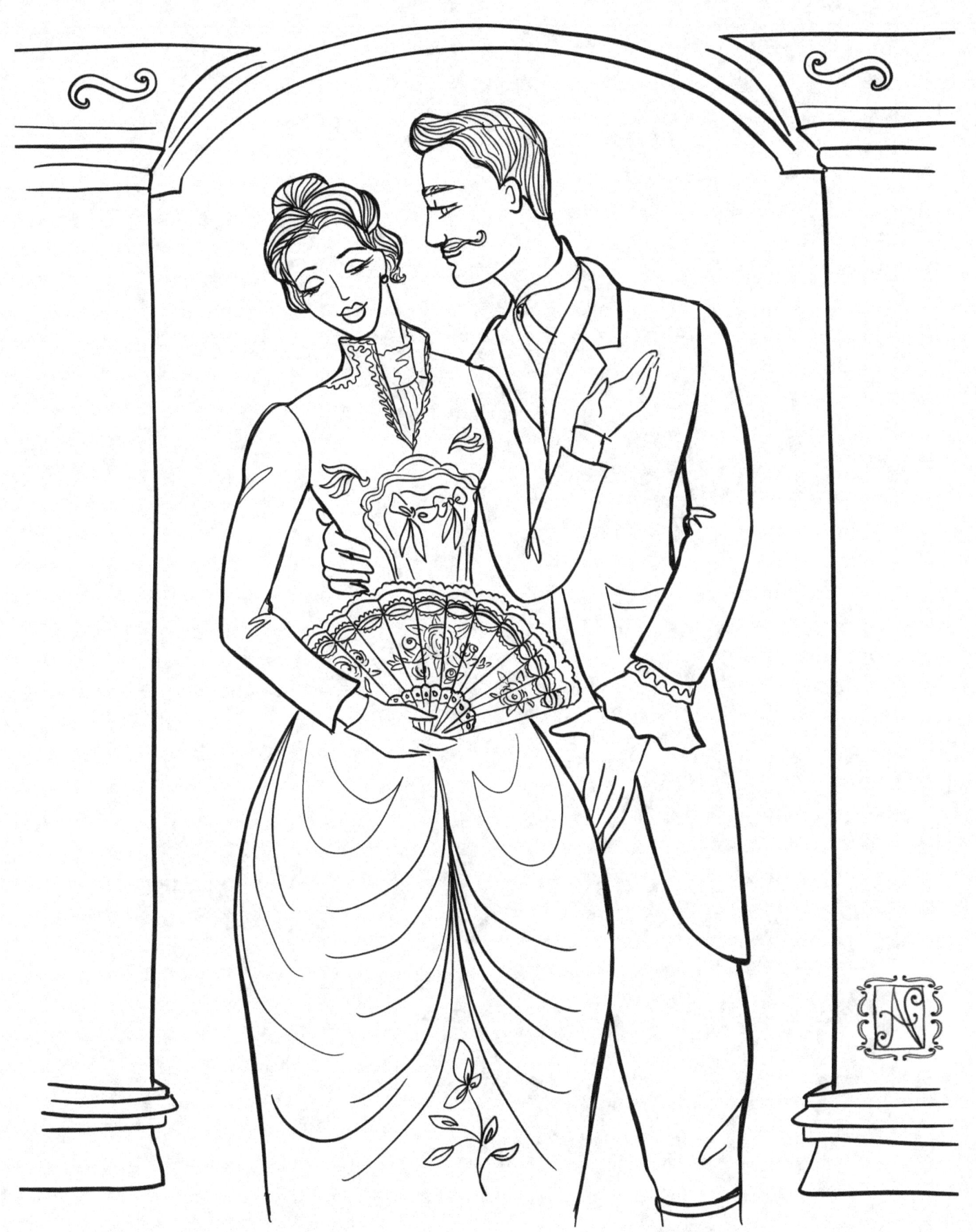

"Nobody minds having what is too good for them."

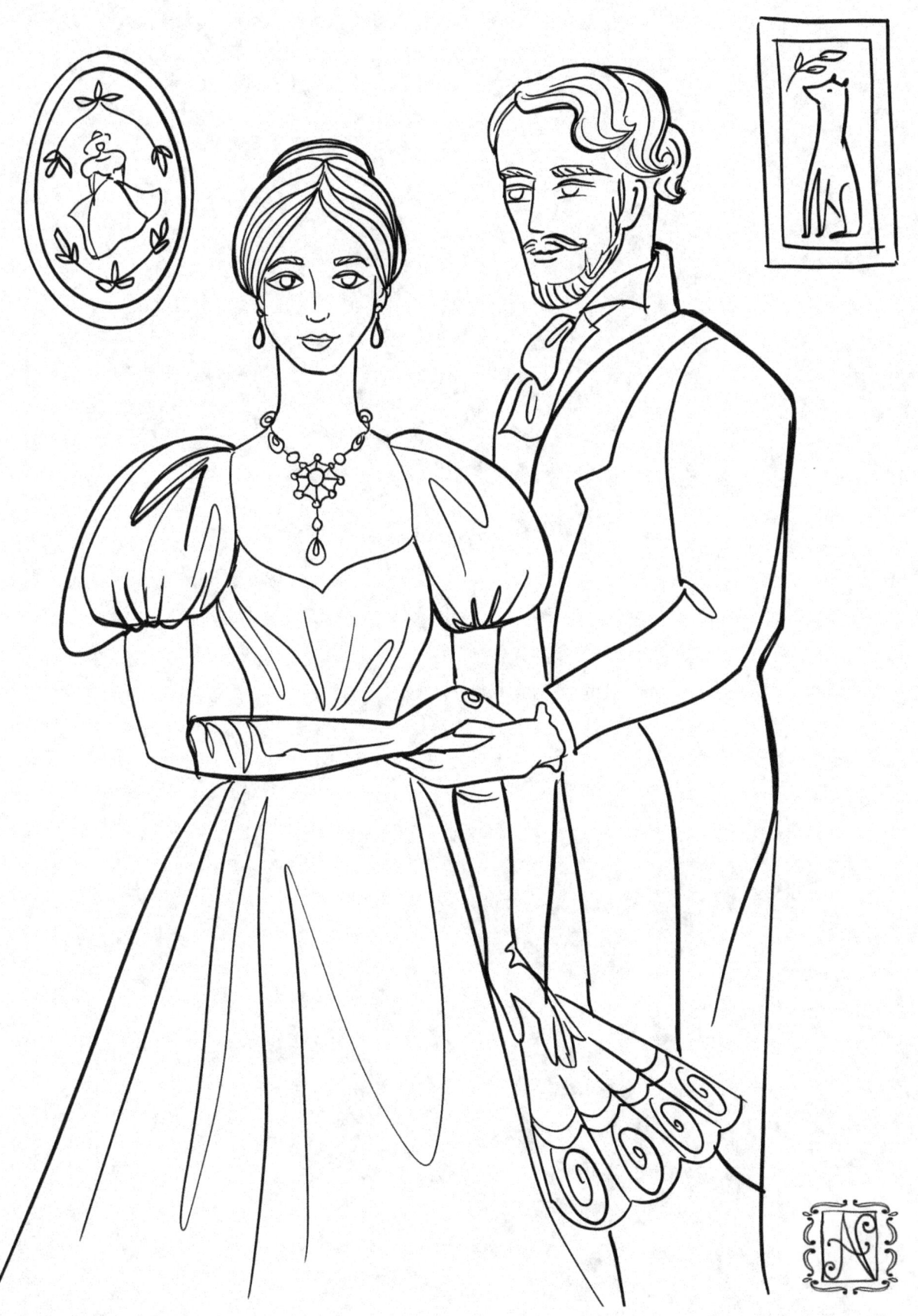

"If I loved you less, I might be able to talk about it more."

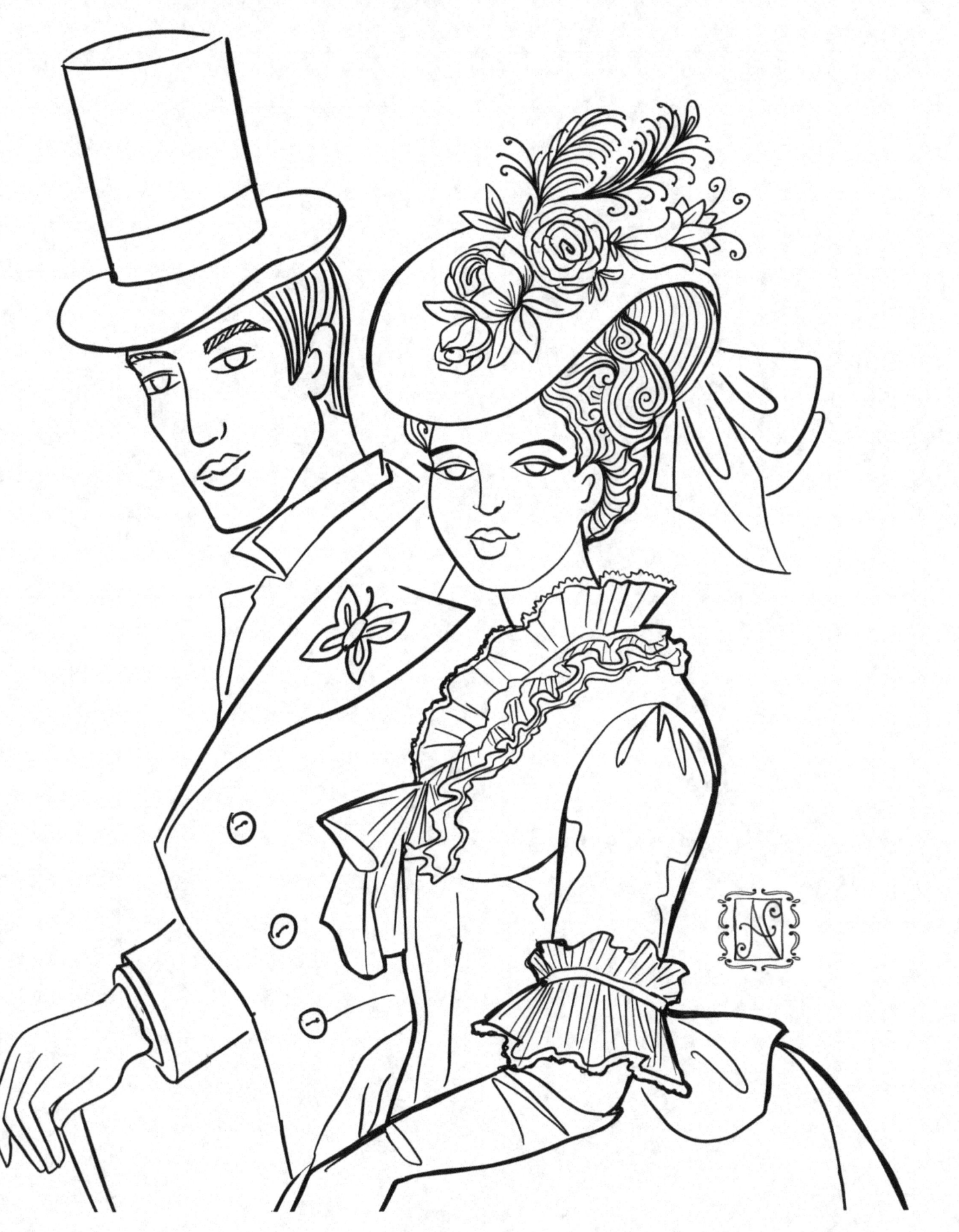

"Indulge your imagination in every possible flight."

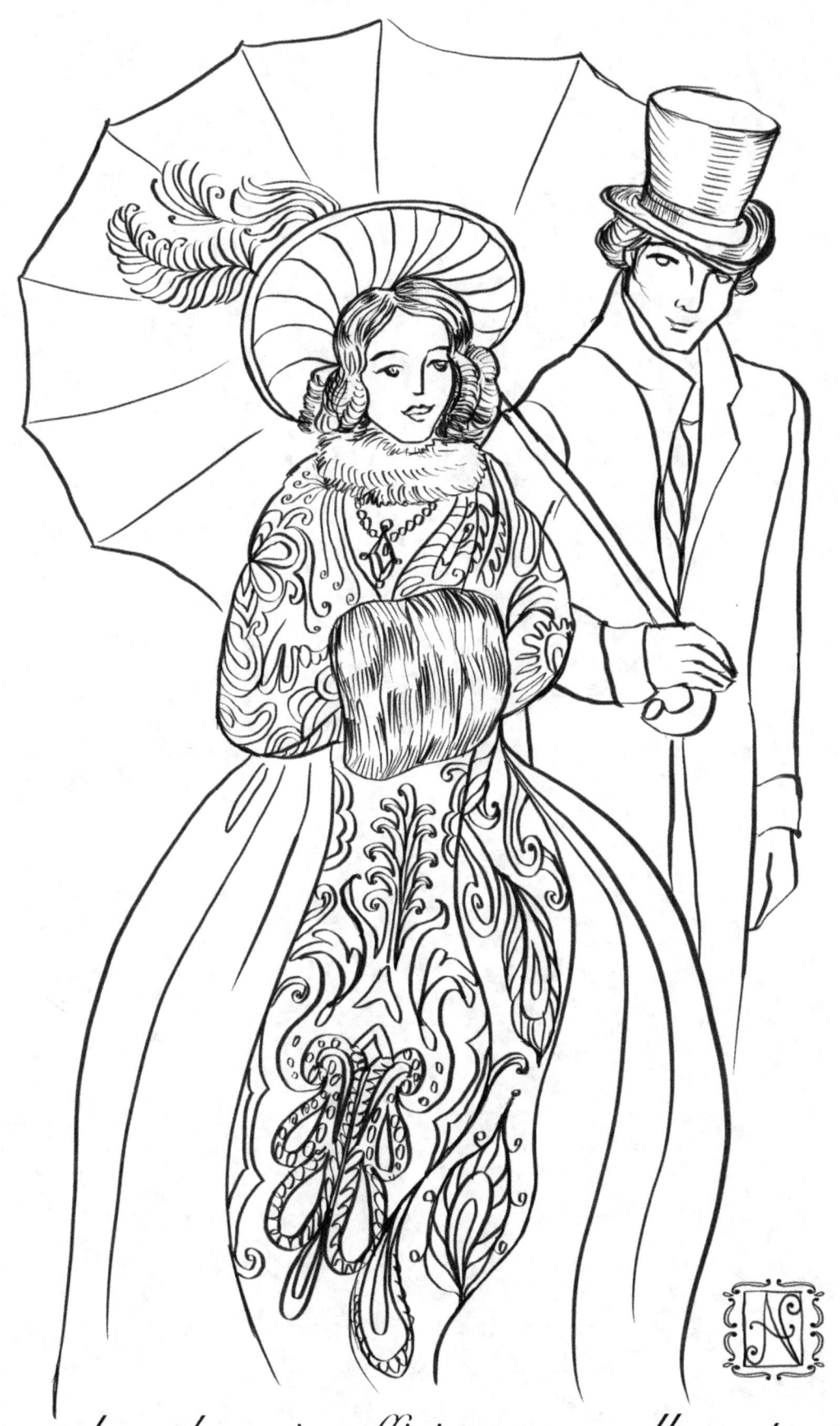

"You showed me how insufficient were all my pretensions to please a woman worthy of being pleased."

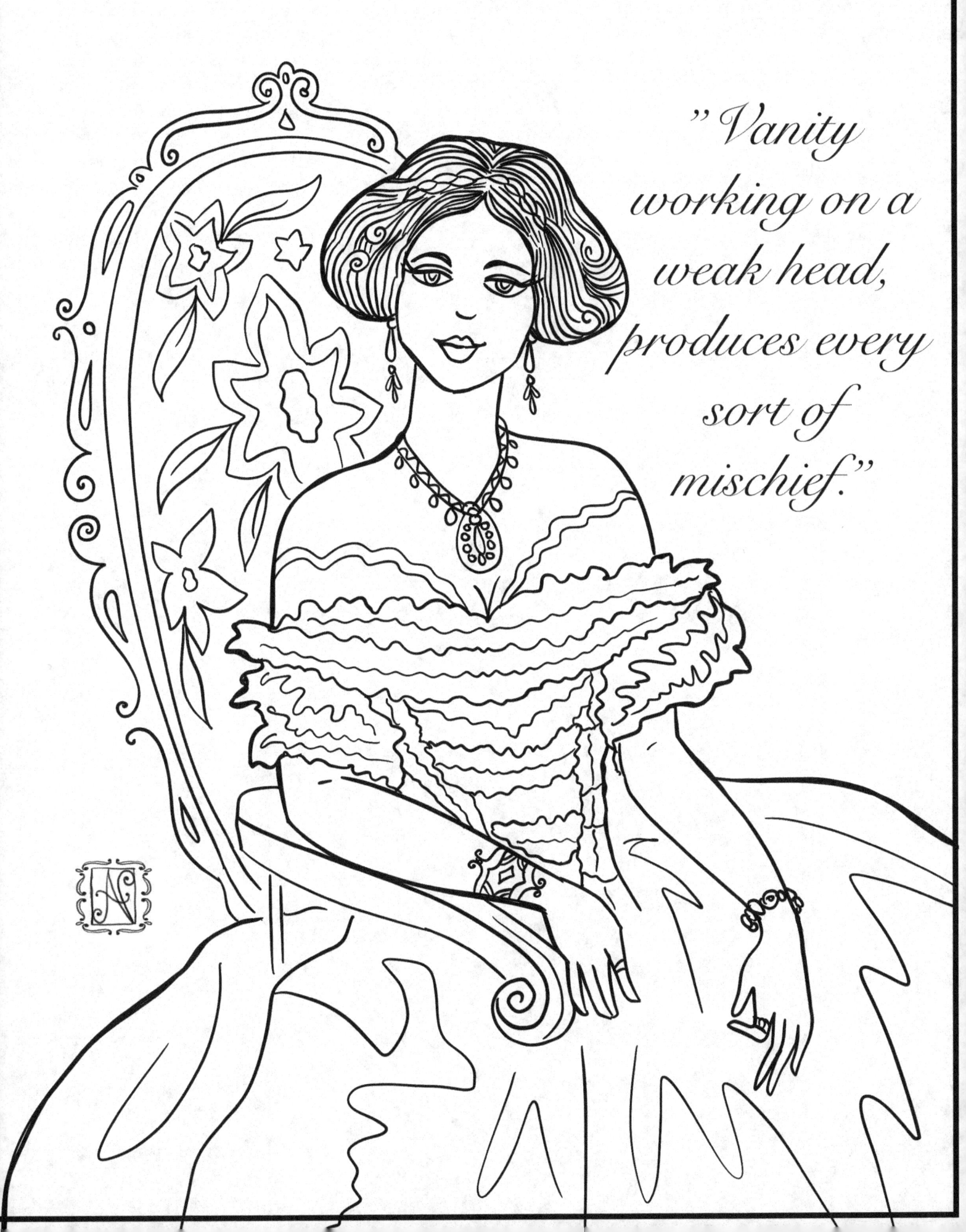

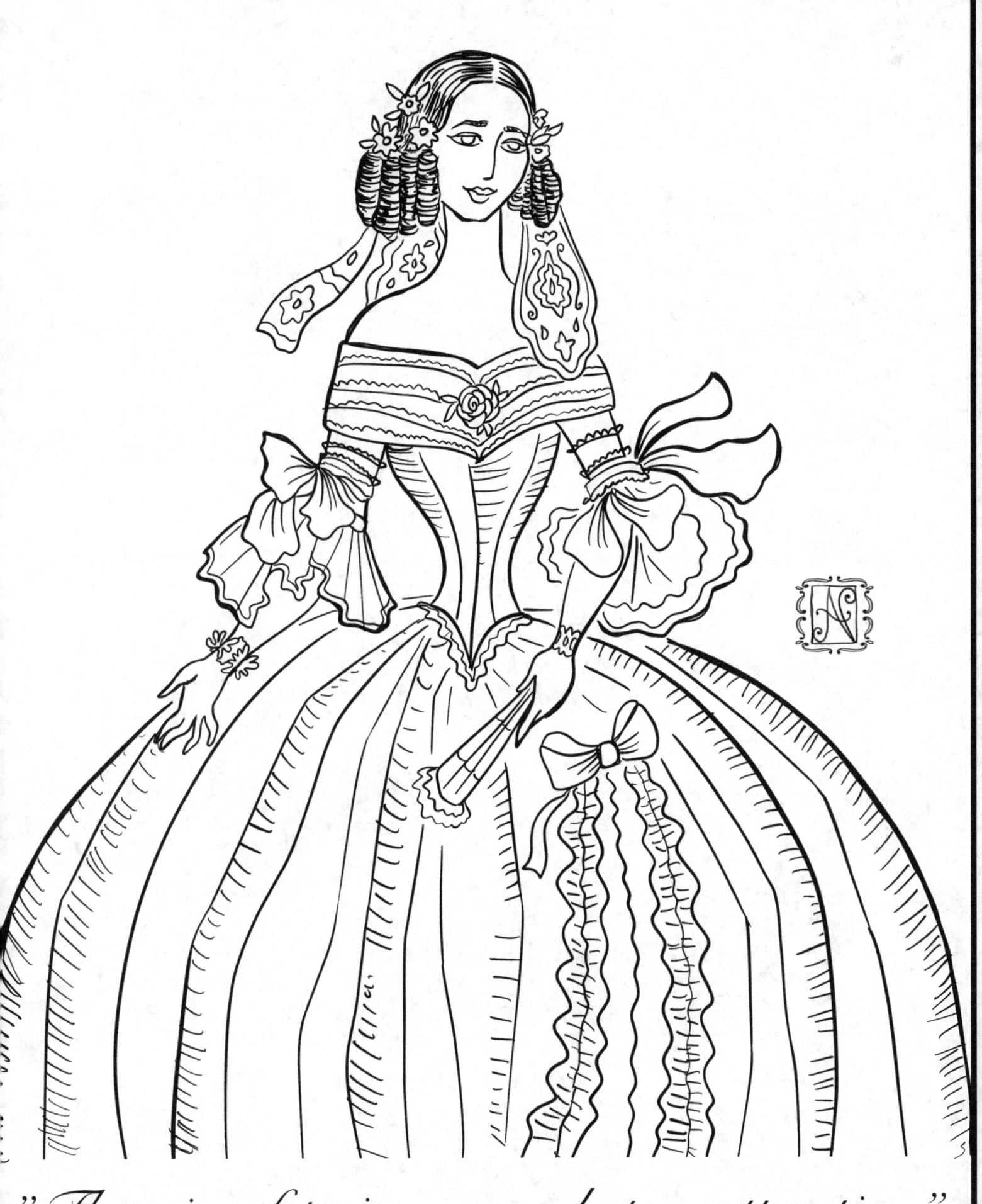

"There is safety in reserve, but no attraction."

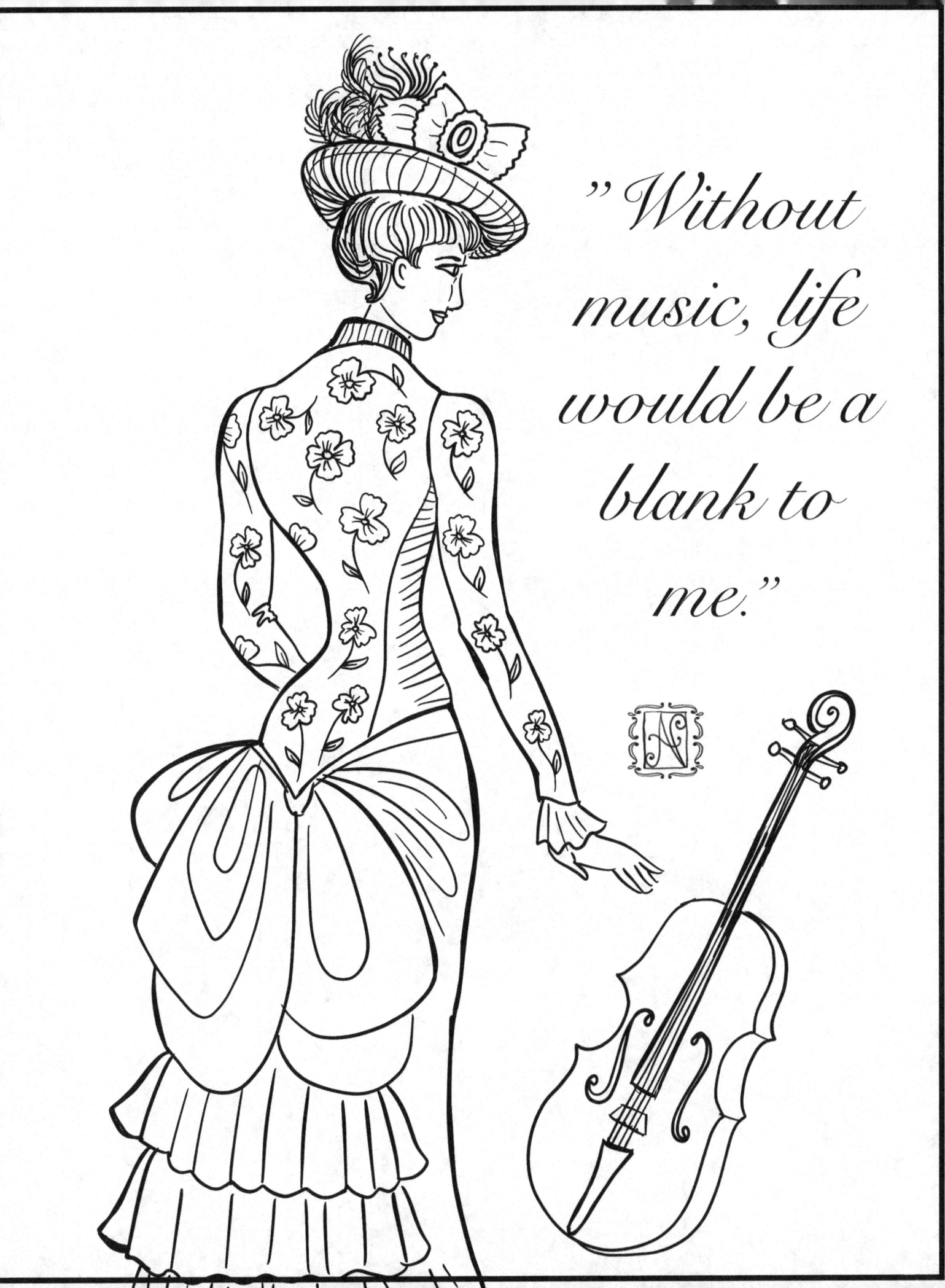

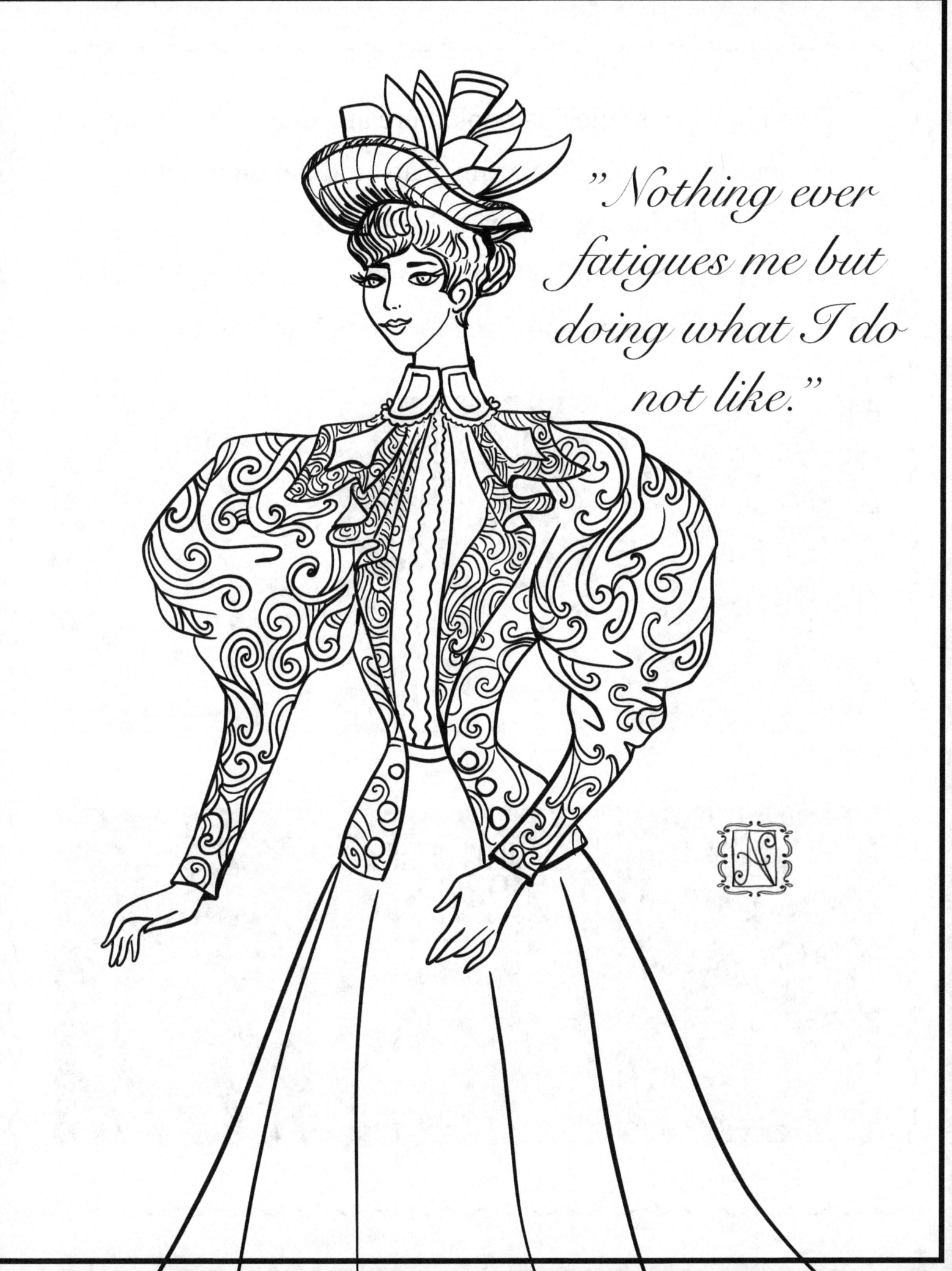

"Nothing ever fatigues me but doing what I do not like."

If you liked this coloring book, here are some more of our books done in a similar intricate and detailed style.
Including "Coloring New York City,"
"The Big Apple Coloring Book," and the "Astrology" series.
You can find them by searching for Anna Nadler on Amazon.

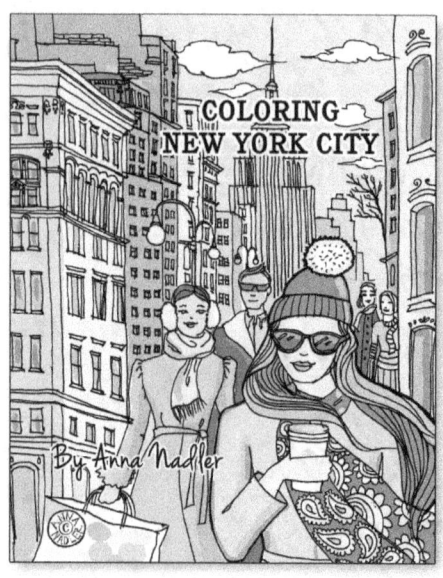
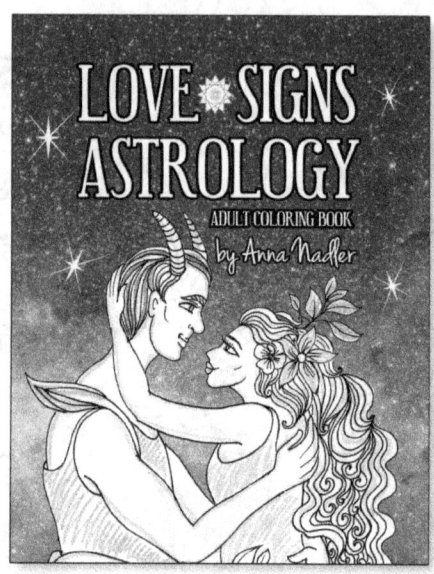
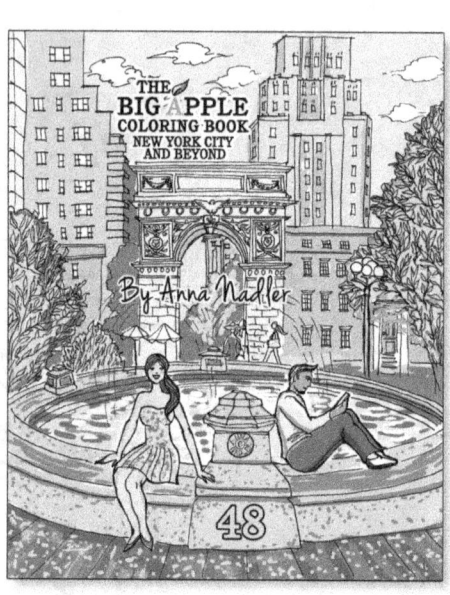
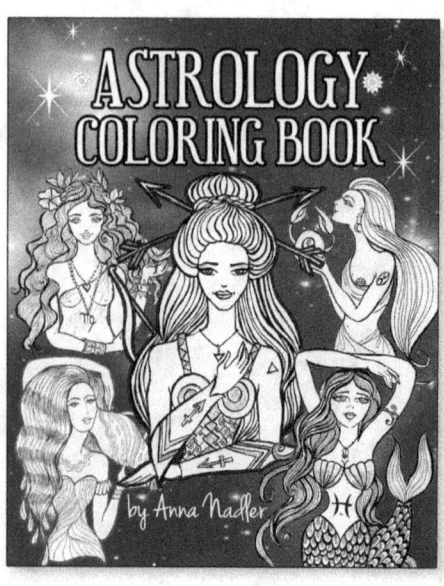
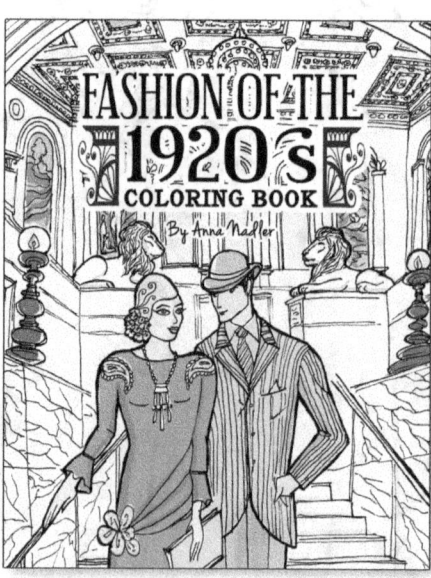
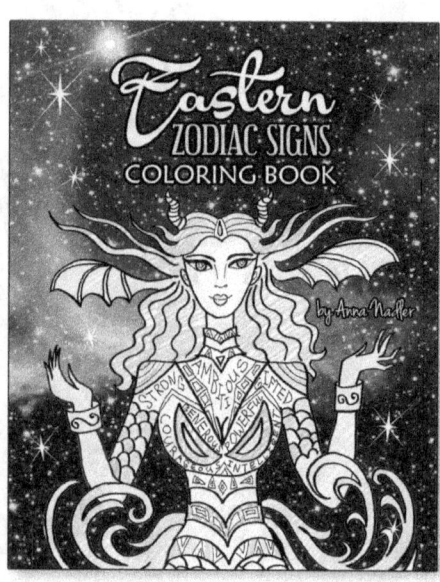

About the Artist

Anna Nadler is an illustrator, graphic designer and author, who lives and works in New York City. She loves drawing fashion, people, animals and architecture, as well as creating unique logo designs for various companies from around the world. You can view more of her work on her website - annanadler.com and on social media platforms. You can also find many of her original art books in her Amazon book store, where she is always adding new coloring books, art tutorials, children's books, gift books, planners and more.
In her free time Anna loves traveling, singing jazz songs and spending quality time with her friends and family.

Thank you for coloring this book!
If you enjoyed it, please leave a review
on Amazon!

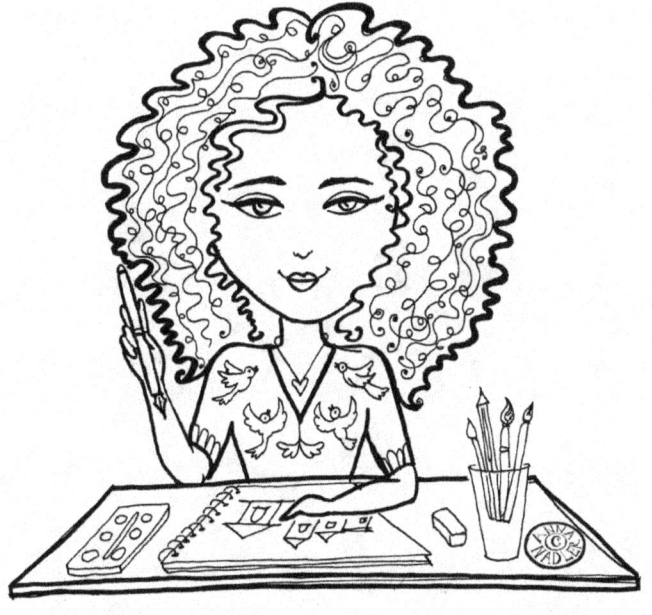

www.ingramcontent.com/pod-product-compliance
Lightning Source LLC
Chambersburg PA
CBHW080517220526
45465CB00006B/2516